Hey LOOK!

I Found the Loose Nut!

A Humorous Look at Customer Situations

from a Technician's View

Scott "Gonzo" Weaver

Hey Look I Found A Loose Nut!
ISBN: 0-88144-430-8
Copyright © 2009 by Scott "Gonzo" Weaver

Published by
Total Publishing and Media
9911 East 54th Street A
Tulsa, OK 74146
www.totalpublishingandmedia.com

DEDICATION

This book is dedicated to all those unsung wrench turners out there who keep the cars, trucks, trains, boats, and R.V.'s on the road for us. Seldom does a thank you ever say enough. Also, an appreciation is in order to everyone in any type of service industry. Those long hours and frustration that amounts to a paycheck at the end of the week is all most of us get in the way of thank you. Your hard work and diligent effort is what keeps the gears turning and this country moving forward. I know this isn't much, but thanks a lot folks. I appreciate it 100%.

TABLE OF CONTENTS

Why read this book?—
Introduction

Have you ever been in a checkout line when somebody in front of you starts to have a fit with the counter person? Have you ever known someone who was telling you a story about how they didn't feel they got what they expected at a retail establishment, but halfway through the story you realized that they didn't have a clue what they were talking about? Did you ever wonder what it was like from the other side of the counter? If you haven't, you should.

As a public service oriented business, it doesn't take long before you run across somebody out there who doesn't have both feet on the ground, or you come across a situation that just doesn't fit the normal day to day routines. Anytime a few plumbers, doctors, lawyers, policeman, or for that matter, any service people get together, they eventually end up talking about work. And it doesn't take long before the subject gets to the "I can top that one!" Every industry can relate to the odd situations that happen from day to day. This book is the kind of thing that might jog your memory of an event in your life or business. Hopefully you will remember them. The funny ones that make you shake your head in disbelief that it actually happened.

This book has many audiences, from the public service worker, to the person too scared to go to any type of repair shop because they are afraid that all service people are just trying to get more money from them with unnecessary repairs. This book is also for the repair guy, who has seen many of these types of situations before. I would love to help bridge that gap between the people who have had bad experiences with repair shops, and help them understand what to look for in a good repair shop, and how to respond to the questions asked by the professional. I'd also like to help the service person become aware that they are not the only person or business to ever run across these sorts of situations.

The people who spend their day at the other end of the phone or behind that counter have families, friends, and homes too. Nobody wants to leave their job in a teeth-grinding-under your breath cussing- and dog kicking attitude. But, some days are like that. I'm very proud of the work and accomplishments that I have done in my life. Running a small business is one of them. And yes, I have gone home with that dog kicking attitude, and really wish it didn't have to be that way. Looking back on those times I realize that "that's life and sometimes things just happen". In some respects, if I had this book to read before hand, I think I would have handled things differently.

I've been in private business for over 25 years, and I'm still amazed that I am able to wake up and go to work each day.

Through recessions and good times, cars have been a part of my life. The automotive field is an ever changing industry, with new styles of cars and trucks and even more complicated systems. There are constant changes in the electronic components and engines which we rely on to get us back and forth to work and for play. It is those systems, and consequently those changes that I am constantly striving to maintain and keep running at a reasonable cost to the consumer.

But, as the never ending changes are made in cars, customers have always remained the same. This is where I went wrong all those years ago, thinking I could run my own business and deal with the general public. Well I have, and now so many years later, I'm about to retire and spend more time fishing, golfing, and watching my grandchildren grow up. I was young (contrary to what my kids believe), and wanted to make a change in what I saw as a problem in the automotive field. Back in the early 80's cars were just starting to come out with computers, and that's how I ventured into owning my own business. If only I knew then, what I know now, I don't know if I would have done it at all. But I did. It's what has brought me the success that I have had over the years and a better understanding of human nature.

I'm not writing this to insult anyone or make fun of anyone. These are the stories, the people, and the events that have graced me with the experiences that I would not have had if it wasn't for owning my own repair shop. Don't get me wrong, some have angered me and some had made me laugh, but looking back on them now, they were all entertaining.

Each one of these stories has some mechanical or electrical information in it. It's not there to show how to repair cars, but only as a reference tool to explain how the story evolved and ended up in this book. These stories are about customers, family, employees, and suppliers. No that's wrong...these stories are about you and me... People.

It all started with just 3 bays in a small shopping center, and of all days to open a business... April 1st....April Fool's day, no less. Hardly a booming place, but it paid the bills. One thing is still true today, the riches in this business can't be measured in the cash drawer, but in the riches of everyday life. People are what make life interesting. Consider yourself lucky to be born in the time when electronics and computers aide our daily lives. It truly is amazing.

The first thing I had to do was to get myself established and make people aware that I was in business. So I took out a small yellow page ad, and off I went into the big world of business.

My first customer was a furniture store. Their Chevy van had a gas gauge that didn't work. Not a big deal, but then again it wasn't a big problem for me, in fact, it was just the type of work I was looking for. Pretty soon the phone started to ring. More and more time passed, and more jobs came through the shop. I did start to notice that not everyone was what I would call "happy" to be at a repair shop. I never saw this before in people. I always did my own repairs, so I never knew that there were places that said they could do a repair but really couldn't. It was quite a shock to me. Somehow doing a good job and getting paid for it didn't exactly set well with some people who were leery of all mechanics.

A lot of them would question your abilities, and whether or not you could actually do what you claimed. You were always facing the problem of being one screw up away from getting your butt chewed out. In some instances you came out as the hero, and everyone walked away with a smile, but other times it didn't work out that way. It's like living on a teeter totter. One side is "genius" and the other side is "idiot," and all day long you are walking back and forth on the board trying to keep the teeter totter balanced and not swaying too much from one side or the other. It's hard to live up to the genius level all the time and I don't think I have to explain about the other side.

Most people will remember a "bad" day at the office or that car repair that went wrong than they do the good times in between. It's not that we dwell on the worst side of life, but misery loves company and everyone has a horror story dealing with a repair on their car or house, but you never hear the stories of how the customers react at the repair shop.

This is what this book is all about. Not so much the highlights and accomplishments of my life, but of the stories and events of the day to day grind of working with the public. I'm sure anybody who has ever had to be at the return desk of a department store, or counter person at a deli, the waiter or waitress at a restaurant, or the lady at the bank in the repo department will relate. Or for that matter, anyone that has had any dealings with customers off of the street, can relate to, or even come up with the same kind of stories. If you have never worked in retail or a service oriented business environment, but you think you know what it's like, then read on. The vision of these stories is from my side of the counter, and how I see you (the consumer) acting out your rage or confusion in front of me. While reading this, you might find some similarities to a situation you've been in. Feel free to sit back with a smile and consider yourself amongst friends because we've all been there. One thing is true, we are all human, mistakes and misunderstandings will happen.

This is a chance to look back on those situations, and see how it looked from the other side.

Meeting different people everyday can be the most rewarding thing you'll ever do. Some will be lifelong customers and friends. Others, you'll wonder how in the world the gene pool didn't drown this one when it had the chance. Every type of person gets their car repaired, from business people to the soccer mom, and that's what makes this kind of profession interesting. You just never know who will walk through the door next. Some of them are unusual to say the least, and others you'll never forget.

These stories are true. They really did happen, even as crazy as some of them sound. Sit back, get comfy, and let me tell you my story. Even the most obvious repairs can have a questionable ending. There are some things I could never quite comprehend. How some people can get into such situations is beyond me. Even now I sometimes feel like that new puppy with his head cocked sideways, and has that "Say what? Are you talking to me?" look on my face.

Read on and see if you agree.

MY WIFE

A few years had passed by since my divorce. My shop had been open about 7 years or so. I was working every day until dark, and watching the kids grow up. I never took a vacation, or any time off. To this day I have taken only a few days off in a row. My business became my life, and not much else did. It seemed as though I blinked, and my daughters were growing up. Then this adventure started.....

That little yellow page ad did make a difference; it also brought me to the true love of my life...my wife. Even today, my wife and I make the joke that if it wasn't for Lee Iacoca we would have never met. You see, she was driving a Chrysler Lebaron, with a lot of miles and a lot of problems.

One day at the shop the phone rang, it was this gal with the Lebaron and a window that didn't work. I said I could fix it and I could get her in the next day. When she came in I was thinking hey, cute chick....wonder if she is married...oh don't go there fella....keep your mind on your work.

I got the keys, pulled the car in and proceed to make the repair. The only thing wrong with it was a small retaining spring in the window motor had broken. I searched all over the shop...couldn't find one anywhere. I went back into the office and went thru my desk draws.....nothing....not a spring to be found. Then I looked over at this beautiful gal......walked over to her with a big smile. She smiled back.

"Is my car ready?"She asked.

I said, "No, but if I could borrow that pen you are using on that crossword puzzle I could fix it right now."

"My pen?" she asked.

"Yes, the pen," I replied. She handed me the pen, and I quickly stripped the pen down to its little pieces and removed the spring. "There, that's all I need. I'll have your car fixed in a jiffy", I told her. I'll never forget the look on her face when I handed her back the pen, minus the spring, of course.

A year or so later she had another problem with her car, but this time she went somewhere else. After several failed attempts by this "other" shop to fix it they finally gave up, and told her to take her car somewhere else. That's when she remembered this goofy guy with the spring. She called me, and as before, "Yes, I can take care of that for you," I told her. Well, it was a little on the strange side as far as repairs goes, but then... this entire book is about strange and unusual experiences..

It turned out that after only 5 or 10 minutes of driving the car it would stall. I had her drive around for a few minutes with a fuel pressure gauge hooked to the engine and held down by the wiper blades. This way she could see the pressure while driving. I kept on working on the other jobs in the shop while she drove around. When she came back and told me what the gauge said when it did stall I had a pretty good idea what was wrong. I grabbed a can of refrigerant and stood by the car making small talk while I waited for the car to die.

We talked about marriage, kids, the shop, weather; you know whatever came to mind. I could tell she was getting very frustrated with her car. The fact that it wouldn't die when it was in the shop was getting her pretty edgy, but she also seemed very interested in talking.

That's when I had an idea. "How about a deal, if I fix your car, you owe me dinner??" She took me up on it. Just then the car died. I opened the hood; shot a quick blast of cold refrigerant at the base of the distributor and told her to start it up. It sprang back to life. A minute later it died again.....another shot of refrigerant. "Start it", and again it came back to life (at this point I look like some sort of genius to her —I'm liking this!).

Her eyes got big and she said, "You know what it is?"

I answered, "Do you know where we are going for dinner?"

"How about Italian?" she said.

"Great, can I pick the restaurant?" I asked.

She said I could. I think I impressed her already. I finished repairing the car, which by the way was a faulty distributor pickup. It just so happened that the restaurant that I chose is the one she had a gift certificate for a free dinner for two. Her boss had given it to her as a going away present. Yes, she was going away. She was on her way to Texas in a few days to attend training for a new job.

She never made it to that job. She stayed, and we were married two months later. A few more years went by, and we decided to have a child. A boy. Mitchell is his name. He takes after his mom. (That's better than the alternative!).

We have a family motto. "It don't get no better" …..Take it anyway you want, but it don't get no better. How she has managed to put up with me for all these years is simply amazing.

Well, I guess it's true then….it don't get no better.

THE DOG STORY

Eventually, after many years I just called all the stories that related to customers explaining the problems with their cars as "dog stories." For example, If someone came in, and I asked the usual question, "What's wrong with the car?" and I didn't get a response like, "my brake lights don't work, the transmission doesn't shift, my engine seems to have developed a miss....Etc...", but instead they started the conversation with a somewhat unrelated saga of their latest adventures—which somehow involved the car....Well, then that's a dog story. Most of the time I would half heartedly listen. I would usually straighten the desk, or scribble some notes if there was something tangible in the midst of the never ending biography. Oh, eventually they would get to the point. Sometimes it took a while and sometimes I may have to scribble out a second note because the first scribble doesn't apply to today's problem. That first problem happened years ago, but, they feel it's necessary for me to know about...EVERYTHING.

If you try to interrupt them in mid story, they'll get off track, usually getting upset, and this whole process takes longer than it was going to take if you would have just shut up and wait till they're done. Then you finally can ask questions regarding the actual repair. Everybody does this in some form or fashion. Most of the time, you don't even know you're doing it. Take for example this story.

This, for the record, is the story that gave this whole thing its name. The Dog Story.....

This was one of those days, where nothing was easy. It seemed every job had some sort of hassle involved. Like, a simple oil change turns into a nightmare, because the bolt is stripped in the oil pan, or the filter was screwed so tight from the last guy that you have to punch a screw driver thru it and use it as a lever to work the filter off. Every job had to be explained in detail, with no mistakes in order to get the correct parts. It was one of those days where details mattered and the fluff wasn't necessary. It just bogged down the daily grind and brought everything to a screeching halt. That was the kind of day I was having when this novelist showed up.

A customer came in; no previous phone call, just a walk in customer. I said "Hello, what can I do for ya today?"

He answered "Well, hello, ya sure can."

"So what is the problem with the car?" I asked, puzzled.

Little did I know that I should sit down and wait this one out. He began his verse and chapter like this;

"Me and my dog were going to my grandmother's funeral up north of here, she was a great lady, blue hair and all, I kind of liked her cooking, but not as much as I like my other grandmother's, but she was always so nice to me. I was making my way to the viewing, north of here, but not too far, sure gets colder up there quicker than it does down here you know. I really hate funerals, dead people and all, I really don't even want to go to my own, but I guess I will, since I'll be the one in the casket you know."

"Well, it began to rain, not hard, but pretty steady, just on and on, some people would call that a drizzle. I don't know about that, it's just rain to me. When I came to some railroad tracks, an old set that's for sure. It didn't have one of those fancy automatic gates and all. It had those railroad 'x' signs with the flashing lights, you know the type. Good thing they still make those; without that flashing light someone could have just zoomed across there and would have never seen a train coming. Just as I crossed the tracks my dog jumped out of the window and then the car died..............

I was intrigued, fascinated, captivated and totally spell bound by this man's detailed description of a day in his life. I couldn't help but sit back for a second and take in this story, of life, weather, animals, and a car. Wow, what a story. Sounded like one of those old country songs. Having the kind of day that I was having, I took a moment and just sat there reliving his story in my head, trying to piece together my scribbled notes and see if there was anything I could use as a diagnostic start of this guy's problem. Let's see, hmm, he went over the railroad tracks on his way to his grandmother's funeral in the rain when the dog jumped out the window.

With all the confusing notes I had in front of me the only thing I could think of to reply with was, "So, how's the dog?"

He looked at me as if he was a deer staring at the headlights. "Huh, what are you talking about? I was talking about my car", he said.

Hey Look! I Found the Loose Nut!

This guy looked like he had enough already, but since my day wasn't going without complications I thought I would play along with his tale of tales. "I know that sir, I replied, I can take care of the car, no problem there, and I am sorry about your grandmother. Sure wish she could give it another try with her cooking. My one grandmother was an excellent cook. Loved to go there when I was little, and the rain, isn't much I can do about that, a slight drizzle is great for flowers, my wife tells me that a lot. Maybe putting the window up would have kept the dog in the car, but you left me hanging here. I'm just wondering what happened to the dog? Did ya go get him? Hmm, I wonder if that's what made the dog jumpy, you know rain and all, or maybe it was the railroad tracks. So where is the dog at now? What kind of dog is it? Have ya had it long? What's the dogs' name? Gosh I love dogs."

Now it was his turn to sit back and ponder. Could it be he forgot a step, missed some important fact, did the dog really jump out of the window, was there even really a dog, did the dog have blue hair???? Was I going to miss the most thrilling moment of all time, because one bit of important information didn't make it in the text of this story? I'm sitting there with anticipation. I could see the deer in the headlights stare has reached the crash point. He answered, "F.U.", and walked out the door, never to be seen or heard from again."

So, I guess I'll never know what happened to the dog or for that matter how well the funeral went, or if it stopped raining. The car … well, I guess some other poor mechanic is going to have to listen to this entire story all over again and maybe get to the bottom of this guy's problem. Or, should I go into more detail?

ARE YOU KIDDING ME?

This is a collection of some of the most unbelievable, zany customer stories I can remember. You just can't make this stuff up! It's some of the most bizarre things I have ever witnessed. How often these stories happen is a mystery, but when they do, you'll never forget them.

"HONK FOR JESUS"

On a very quiet afternoon the phone rang. "Good morning can I help you?"

"Yes, I'm having a problem with my horn," the lady said. "It's staying on by itself, so my husband unplugged the horn to make it stop, but I was wondering if you could fix it?"

"Sure can ma'am," I said. "Can you drop it off today or tomorrow?"

"Tomorrow, great, I'll see you then."

The next day the lady came to the shop, carrying a bible under one arm, and sporting a huge bee hive hairdo. "Here's the keys, call me when it's repaired." she said.

I started working on it right away. As I was checking it out, I noticed that the upper right corner of the horn pad was bent down just a tiny bit. After plugging the actual horn back in I reached in and pulled up on the horn pad. Sure enough the horn shut off.

Now, this is back before the introduction of air bags, but the manufacturers were making attempts to make room on the cars, so that in the event they went into production less work was needed to retool the existing models. Some of you may remember when the horn pads were these large boxy types in the center of the steering wheel, while other manufactures had moved the horn entirely from the center of the steering wheel all the way over to the turn signal stalk where you pushed it in towards the steering column to activate the horn. This was one of those "boxy" types.

As I was "un bending" the horn pad, I had the key on so the steering wheel would be unlocked. I couldn't help noticing the radio station it was tuned to. It was a religious channel, and just about then the preacher came on and said, "If you're out there in your car, and you hear my voice, praise Jesus, Praise Jesus....Honk your horn if you love Jesus. Hallelujah!! Amen, praise Jesus." I didn't think anything of it, just went on with the job at hand.

I called the lady, and told her that the car was ready. She then informed me that their other car has the same problem. Could I fix that one too?

I said, "Sure, bring it when you pick up your other car." She stopped by later and traded out cars.

The wildest thing was that it was exactly the same type car—same color, same year, same everything, and ...now don't get ahead me.......the exact same problem.

It didn't take long before I called her back to tell her what I found, but instead her husband answered. He told me how they had bought both cars at the same, and sometimes in a rush he would grab the wrong car in the morning. "That's great. Well, this one is already to pick up", I said. "Oh, and I guess you should tell her not to smack the horn so hard when she is "honking for Jesus."

There was a long pause on the phone. In a deep baritone voice coming through the phone, "Ahhhh, that's actually my fault," he said, "I already got chewed out from the wife. She thought it was my fault all along. I would appreciate it if you wouldn't mention that again. I'll be by later to pick it up."

Later that day, while in the office doing paper work, the door opened. This huge man came through the door. He had to stoop over, and use one shoulder at a time to get through the door. As he managed to get his massive frame through the door, he stood up straight. He was taller than the door itself; his hands were the size of dinner plates. (Good God, I thought he was one of those pro wrestler guys or something). The man jokingly said, "I'm here to pick up my car, the one with the Jesus marks on the horn pad."

This guy was the biggest man I have ever seen. He was a football defensive line all by himself. His thumbs had to be an inch thick. I couldn't think of anything to say. The sheer size of this man was enough to make me speechless. It's not every day a walking billboard comes through your door asking about his car with Jesus marks on it. I had to have been staring at this guy for some time by now. I know I must look shell shocked to the guy. I couldn't think of much to say except for, "Sir, you can honk that horn anyway you like. I can fix it again and again. It would be my pleasure to fix it for you anytime you would like. Feel free to bang on the horn all you want." He laughed at the whole situation. Paid his bill and got in his car honking the horn as he left.

The Lord works in mysterious ways. I just hope he has a sense of humor.

YOU'RE CAR SMELLS BAD, REALLY BAD.

The smell coming from this car was so bad you couldn't get away from it. As I walked to the car this stench permeated the air around it. I was supposed find the problem with the turn signals on this Cadillac. I believe it was a mid 80's. The car absolutely reeked. I held my breath as I pulled it in. Jumped out of the car long enough to catch my wind. Even with the door closed it stunk, but I had to get back in there to check it out. One breath at a time I managed to get the diagnosis done. It's a faulty turn signal switch inside the steering column. Just great. Now I'm hoping he will pass on the repair so I don't have to get back in there. Nope......he wants it done. As I was getting my nerve up to get back in there I found where all this smell was coming from. It was coming from the back seat. In a couple of grocery bags were about a 100 ribeye steaks....fermenting.....yuk. Turns out this guy owns a well known steak house. It was enough to make your eyes water. But it was my job for the day. To make matters worse, this was one of those telescopic steering wheels. These types require a little extra effort to get the steering wheel off. Great, just what I needed. Believe it, or not I did 99% of this job with my head outside the car, and only dove under the dash long enough to get it disconnected and the new parts installed.

After managing to get the new switch installed and checked, I got behind the wheel one more time and pulled the car to the far end of the parking lot. I called the owner, and told him that I had the repairs made. And, by the way, there is this awful smell. His reply,"What smell?" Good God, I just can't believe it. Small flocks of birds were diverting their flight paths away from that end of the parking lot. Off he went in his stink mobile, as happy as he could be. Anybody hungry?

COOKIE BARF

Ok, maybe I didn't handle this one as well as I should have, but this is how it went down. A lady came in with a mid 80's Cougar with electric seat and power window problems. On these cars, the seat and window switches are on the center console instead of on the door panels. It does give it a cleaner look on the door panels, and it eliminates the old problem of having rain getting into the window switches. However, in this case I think I would have rather had them on the door panels.

When I got into the car to bring it in the shop, I instinctively reach for the center console area to move the seat back or try a window. Looking down for the switches I notice I couldn't see them. Not only were the switches hidden, but for that matter half of the entire console was covered with thick, smelly goo. It looked like some kid or a dog had thrown up all over the console. Not a little bit mind you, a lot of barf. It had to be at least an inch thick of gooey, gelled barf with edges drying to a crackly cement texture. This wasn't that fresh but it wasn't that old….totally disgusting.

I didn't even move the car. I walked straight into the waiting room, and asked the lady if she would mind getting her car cleaned before I worked on it. The vomit was right in the area that I had to work. I also told her that it can't be that healthy driving around with this stuff in her car. Not to mention the fact that the console's finish is probably ruined by all the body fluids and acids present in that nasty stuff. I was shocked at her answer.

She was sitting in a reclining chair in the waiting room reading a book. She seemed very calm and unconcerned . Never once looking up from her book, and as nonchalantly as I've ever seen, she said, "You can open the doors and take a garden hose to it for all I care."

"No really ma'am, you've got to get it cleaned, or I may take you up on that garden hose idea. I just can't work with that stuff oozing through the switches and under the console. You know, that stuff will be in every crack and crevasse that you can think of," I said.

Still, she looked at her book and with only an occasional glace up at me, she replied, "Okay, fine. I don't care if you get the seats wet either."

"Ok, lady," I answered. "Doors open, and a shot of water across the seats coming up."

I pulled the car right in front of the lobby window were she could see the whole thing. I knocked on the window, as a last chance offer to change her mind. Without a reply or look up from her book, I turned the hose to the car and like a tidalwave, I proceeded to flood the console area. All that goo and yuck was flushed across the passenger seat and out the door. I calmly rolled the hose up and walked back inside. I didn't even bother to diagnose it. Let's face it, it's now water damaged. I called the dealer for a price check on replacement switches and gave the lady the estimate, including the Chinese fire drill wash job. She said do it.

I ordered the parts, installed them, and everything worked just fine, even though a lot of that goo had trickled down into the connectors as well. But I managed to clean it up too, and got the lady back on the road. I left my towels in the car. I thought it was considerate of me....or maybe the wet towels and cookie barf mix could just ride off into the sunset with her.

ANGRY AND I'M NEVER COMING HERE AGAIN

A retired lady, who had been in several times before, needed a brake job on her little Buick. I said sure, why not, I could do that for her. She was a nice gal, late 50's early 60's, sharp as a tack. I put the car up on the lift, checked it out, and gave her an estimate. The little lady waited in the lobby for me to finish with the brake job. She talked a bit with my wife, and was very friendly towards all the staff and other customers who came in and out of the lobby.

I finished the brake job with a trip around the block to make sure everything was working just fine. I didn't notice anything wrong, and parked it out front for her. But the next day I was in for a whole new side to this lady.

As soon as she opened the lobby door she started in on me. "You've got a problem to take care of!" she angrily told me. "That problem is me! After I left here yesterday my car has made a noise every time I hit the brakes! Now what are you going to do about it? I expect things to be right, and you are not going to get away with screwing up my car! I'll have you know I have connections in this town." She ranted on. "I'm never coming back here again. To think, all the work I have given you, and now this! You are the worst mechanic I have ever been to."

Wow, what can I say, what can I do? This lady is putting up a frontal assault and I have no choice but to defend my honor. Dare I brave this gauntlet? Should I even speak? Or should I bow and ask for mercy? I chose…. "Let me take it around the block once ma'am and see what I can find out."

She insisted on going along so I could be finger poked at the moment the noise happened. Oh there was a noise all right. It was coming from the passenger seat. And yes, there was a "thump, clank, clank, clank, thump, thump" when the brakes were applied. This lady never shut up all the way around the block. I used exactly the same course I drove the previous day just to be sure I didn't miss anything. I couldn't wait to get back to the shop. My arm was sore from all the poking, not to mention ringing in my ears.

At the shop, we both got out of the car. I went directly to the trunk. She was right there with her no-stop verbal abuse. I opened the trunk and there was the noise. A loose 6 pack of soda was sloshing around in the trunk, namely the thump, the clunk.

I asked her "Did you happen to go grocery shopping after you left my shop yesterday?

"Why, yes I did." She answered. "But what does that have to do with my brakes?" I handed her the sodas and told her that this was what was making the noise. If she would like to drive around the block one more time while holding on to the soda cans I could prove it to her.

Nope, she wasn't buying that. I believe she was more upset with herself. All I got was that look my kids would give me when you catch them with the cookies, and they deny being in the cookie jar. The lady never said another word to me. She put the sodas on the front seat and drove off.

I hope those sodas went down just fine. A little apology would have been nice. Na, drink up lady, I understand.

EARLY MORNING DE-LIGHT

I had a nurse come into the shop one afternoon. She had just finished her morning shift at the hospital. She told me that things were kind of tight at her house financially, and didn't have a lot to spare for car repairs. I told her I would help her out as much as I could.

Her problem was that her headlights didn't work, and she really needed to take this old Datsun back and forth to work every day, regardless if she got a ticket for no headlights. "I get the picture ma'am. I'll take a look at it." I said. In came this decrepit piece of has been machinery that looked like it should have been crushed years earlier. All rusted and dented up with not much left of the interior. But as it was, this was this ladies only ride to and from work.

I got right to work finding the problem. It wasn't that hard to find. At the positive battery post on this type of car was a series of fusible links that powered up different systems in the car. One of them was corroded off the terminals. It just so happen to be the one that powered up the headlight system.

I grabbed the trusty old baking soda, and cleaned off the crud from the positive post of the battery. After replacing the corroded end of the fusible link, I attached it back onto its proper post. One flick of the headlight switch and she was in business.

I went into the lobby and told the lady what I had found. I told her that it was going to be a cheap fix, and not to worry about having to get a loan (as she had thought she needed) to get the car fixed. I then asked her how long has she been driving around with no headlights. Since she had already told me that she had to leave for work in the early morning hours to get to work on time, I was thinking she had some sort of route that would keep the prying eyes of the law off of her tail. She replied. "Oh I had headlights all the time; I just wanted the factory ones to work because I was getting tired of changing the batteries in the other ones." Say what????? Did I miss something here? I thought I was pretty good at reading the electrical systems. What did I miss on the electrical schematics that she was aware of, and I wasn't?

"Really?" I said. "Can you show me what you are talking about?"

She walked out to the car and there on the edge of the front bumper were two 9 volt flashlights duct taped with what could have been a whole roll of tape. She walked right up to them and pushed the button on the right and left flashlight. Then she turned around to face me with both arms out stretched like a T.V. ad model; pointing one toe and all. And wouldn't you know it...she's got headlights. "I just thought it was going to cost so much to fix that I have been putting it off for months." She said. "But I have had to buy so many batteries I thought it would be cheaper to find out what was really wrong with them."

Now I'll admit, I don't think I have ever seen duct taped flashlights on a bumper before. And I haven't seen them since. But I'll tell you this, if I'm ever in the need of a nurse who can think on her feet, and get the job done till the cavalry comes to save ya......this is my gal...way to go girl, you've got my vote

HOW NOT TO GET ON YOUR MECHANIC'S BEST SIDE

This lady not only had an intermittent problem, but an attitude to go along with it. Her story starts out with a tow truck dropping off her van. I don't know what kind of van, as I never saw the van. This lady walks into my lobby and in a very cheery smile starts to tell me all about her van.

It was having some sort of problem with the fuel system, or at least that's what the last mechanic thought it was. Besides, that mechanic had just installed a new fuel pump, so she was sure that wasn't the problem. (I'm never sure of anything until I see the failure myself.) Then she told me about the guy before that who thought it was an ignition problem, and a new distributor didn't fix her problem either. Of course there was the first guy who looked at it, oh, and he thought it just needed a tune-up.

It was several minutes of discussion about the van, the mechanics, and the usual small talk you run into with most people. I explained to her about how I would take on the job based on the fact that it was intermittent and of course, I just don't start throwing parts on a job, I want to see the car fail and then diagnose it. I'm sure the other shops were seeing failures based on the condition of the van and probably had valid reasons for the work they did.

She was fine with that you see, because she was still in the process of suing the last three repair shops for not doing what they said they were going to do, and that is "fix the car". I asked her if she had ever taken it back to them to see if they would take another look at the van. No, she wasn't going to do that. She wanted to sue everybody involved and put them all out of business. She was very serious about this whole suing thing, and quite happy to tell me all about it. Needless to say I was getting a little nervous.

I told her that wasn't exactly going to happen, people make mistakes, things happen and you need to expect that with an intermittent problem. That, she could agree on. She understood it wasn't going to be easy to find a problem that wasn't there all the time. But she heard good things about me, and thought she would take one more chance at getting the van repaired before giving up on it. I was finally going to get her name on a work order when she mentioned one more thing to me...... If I didn't get it fixed, she was going to sue me too. Time out, back this wagon up partner, game over, stop the presses. I threw my pen down on the counter, and with a stern voice just slightly under yelling volume I said, "Get OUT lady, and take your van with you!"

Now, I need the work, hell the shop was dead. But, I don't need a noose over my head while I'm trying to solve a problem that 3 other repair shops failed to find the first time around. Who's to say that the work already done wasn't entirely needed? Who's to say that the van was worse off than she believes it to be? I'm not sure I needed that kind of pressure. I'm not sure if I needed the paycheck that much. I think I'm just going to sit here and watch cars drive by, because I don't think I want to spend any more time with this lady or her car.

MOVIE STAR

There is one thing that can ruin a car more than anything else; it's the lack of proper maintenance. So many people will just drive their car until a catastrophic failure occurs, and then expect that to be the only thing that will need to be fixed. As a car ages more components will start to break down, gaskets can shrivel up and bolts can come loose. Even rubber and plastic will break down after several years. But there is a way to make things last longer. MAINTENANCE! ! ! Keeping it clean, and keeping up on the general maintenance can reduce the amount of failures you'll have. The harder you are on a vehicle, say like towing or high mileage usage the more likely you will need some additional maintenance. When you see a minor problem, get it repaired as soon as possible. That way it doesn't have a chance to turn into a much larger problem. If you buy a used car—cheap used car—chances are you are buying something that needs some sort of service done to it.

Hey Look! I Found the Loose Nut!

This is just what happened with a rundown early 80's Escort came in one day. The guy had bought it to drive as a work car, and the previous owner told him that it was a great car and never had any problems with it. Neglected, was the best way to put it. This was a typical neglected vehicle that I would see in the shop. Oil leaks, coolant leaks, bad hoses and belts and several dings, crushed fenders and broken glass. Not the kind of car you wanted to take on a cross country trip, let alone across town.

I myself don't like to work on these worn out scrap heaps because they almost always end in a bad way. This was no exception. The tired old Escort came in with a drivability problem. The carburetor driven engine was old and tired with about 130 thousand miles on the odometer. You definitely wouldn't say it ran like new in any shape or form. There was no doubt that it had been run hard all of its life. In between the seats there were piles and piles of green rubber bands and plastic bags. This guy was using this car to deliver papers for sure. An honest job, tough hours, and little pay, but it's also tough on a vehicle. They just don't hold up under this kind of abuse.

We started it up in the shop and let it run for awhile. It seemed to idle just fine, and even rev out pretty good. That is, if you could stand the smell of the burning oil. You could keep busy for a week on just the problems you could see on the surface let alone what might be lurking under the inch of greasy dirt on the engine. After shutting it off and checking the oil we couldn't see much more to do except take it for a ride and see what we could find out. The tires were good and the brakes looked solid so we thought we would give it a try.

Everybody at the shop knows there is a particular route we always take just in case a customer's car breaks down, and we need a tow back or need some help from the guys in the shop. Thankfully we had that going for us because after the tech left on the drive, he never made it back when he should have. I jumped into the service truck and headed down the road. I found him walking back not too far from the shop. He told me that the timing belt broke, so it wasn't going anywhere until we got a tow truck to bring it back to the shop.

Towing it back to the shop led to a tear down of the timing cover. Sure enough the timing belt was broken, and a good reason why was found. The belt was original and covered in wear cracks and oil. The oil was from the crankshaft seal. Normally the belt would have been changed on a predictable time table, however, this guy didn't have the time… he just drove the poor thing. It was just a matter of time before it was going to break free. Luckily this is what is called a "non-interference" engine, meaning, the valves and the piston will not touch each other if the belt breaks.

I called him and he was quite understandably upset, I knew he would be. He came in with a running pile of crap and now he has a pile of crap that isn't running. I offered to help him out since it did occur while we had it on a test drive, but I also wanted to make sure he understood that the lack of maintenance was the real issue. He understood and wanted to come down and get some pictures of it. "Sure, that would be great." I said.

The next thing I know is this guy comes in the front door of the lobby with a video camera on his shoulder and is taping away as he narrated this episode of "car broken at the repair shop". Oh, and I knew who was going to be the star of this episode…me. This wannabe movie director/investigative reporter had all his questions pre-rehearsed. The only problem was he had already thought he knew the answers. You could tell he had rehearsed his half of the conversation and thought he had the answers already figured out.

The only thing he didn't count on was his leading star to be so damned defensive. "So what caused the timing belt to fail?" he asked.

"Your lack of proper care and the lack of routine maintenance caused the failure." I answered.

"So, so you think I drove it around and broke the belt, so, so it wasn't your tech driving it too fast that caused it, aye?" he stuttered.

"No, it wasn't that," I calmly answered back. "Cars and trucks are made to take the abuse of everyday use, and are very good at handling the strains that we put them under. The difference is that we forget to take in account the amount of wear and tear we put on a vehicle during its lifetime. That's why the manufacturer gives us an owner's manual with a maintenance schedule. In it is a schedule that will help keep the car in the best shape possible. Failure to do that can end in premature failure or even worse."

He didn't have any answer for that. He tried, but the words kept getting in the way of his mouth.

Then I asked him. "Since this is on film, can you tell me when you performed your last oil change, or the last time you had it serviced at all? No? Then, when is the last time you had the tire pressure checked, or are you aware of all the oil leaks you have? Let's go look at the car."

The camera was shut off by then, I guess he thought it wasn't looking good for him or because it wasn't going the way he thought it was. For all I know, the batteries might have been going dead and he needed to save the rest for the next movie adventure.

Can't say for sure what his plans were. All I know is we put the belt on and gave him the usual warning that unless he had the front seal replaced he wasn't going to stay on the road much longer. I'm sure he didn't listen, I'm sure he isn't going to be making any great epics out of his little movie. So I guess that was my turn at being in front of the camera, maybe next time I'll wipe the grease off first. I'm not a movie star ...... I'm just a mechanic.

BOTTOM SHOCKER

Now here is a story to spark your interest. A customer called and said he just purchased a car from the police auction, and had some sort of strange noise coming from the driver side electric seat. Seems every time he moved it there was a strange electrical sound. He thought it was something wrong with the seat motor. Being an electrical repair shop he figured he was coming to the right place to get it fixed. "Sure," I said. "What kind of car is it?"

"It's a Peugeot." He answered.

I'm not much on a Peugeot, but I told him I can take a quick look at it and see if I can do anything for him.

A day or so later the car arrived at the shop. After pulling it into a bay I tried the driver's seat. Sure enough, as you moved the seat forward an inch or two a loud horrible buzzing of electricity emanated from under the seat. Roll the seat back and the noise would stop. Well then, what to do? I decided to roll the seat forward to the spot that made the noise. It seemed to be pretty consistent, same place, same noise.

When I moved the seat to the spot that made the noise I got out of the car and looked underneath. The noise immediately stopped ...nothing, not a hint of any noise or strange buzzing. The car had all black interior, black seats, black carpet; even the seat rails and brackets were all black. It looked fine to me, of course it's still a Peugeot, and I just don't go poking my head under Peugeot seats every day, so I must be missing something.

I rolled the seat forward and back several times and still no noise. What in the world is going on? I called over my helper and told him "Listen to this, see what you think." The noise was still gone. I explained to my helper what I had found. He was at a loss himself. I climbed back in the car and sure enough as long as I was sitting in the car it would make the noise. Get back out of the car and try it, nothing. Sit in the car and the noise did it every time. This is ridiculous, I heard the sound myself, and I'm not going crazy, am I? I got out again, but this time I had my helper get in and move the seat. He moved the seat forward and within a few inches it starting making the noise. I told him to lift his butt out of the seat...the noise stopped. He tried several times; I tried a couple of times. We didn't think anything of it. Actually we were having fun with it. One of us would sit in the seat and make a fake pistol with our fingers as if we were shooting each other. Raise and lower our butts in and out the seat and play like we were Buck Rogers or something. "Ok, enough fun, sit back down," I said, "I'll look underneath this time." I got down to where I could look under the seat at about the same time he was putting his weight back into the cushion.

Just then I saw the problem. Oh my! I had to look again and again just to make sure I was seeing what I thought I was seeing. My helper asked. "What is it?" with great surprise and anticipation. As I looked underneath the seat I could see a perfect bluish white lightning bolt about an inch or so long. It was pointed right at the bottom of the cushion but only a fraction of an inch from the metal bracing of the seat. In a very calm voice I softly told him. "Now listen carefully, I want you to raise your butt out of the seat, and I'll move the seat towards the rear. There is a police taser pointing at your ass right now. Move very carefully, and I don't think you'll get shocked." I think I shook him up a bit. But he carefully lifted his weight out of the seat.

The taser was the exact same color as the carpet and under side of the seat. It was so well camouflaged that it appeared to a part of the seat mechanism. If it wasn't for the lightning bolt I don't think you could have spotted it. It really looked like a part of the seat brackets. After moving the seat back, the taser eased off of the button and came back to rest with the business end pointing harmlessly away from his "derriere". I then could reach under the seat and pull the butt buzzer out from under the seat.

I called the customer and told him what I found. To say the least he was shocked. So were we for that matter…well, almost.

NO APOLOGY NECESSARY

Another day at the shop started out like any other day at the shop. Until the phone rang. It was one my old customers who had been in the shop several times with this old mid 70's LTD. It had a dent down the passenger side from the front to the back, as if it had careened off another car. This guy practically lived in it. There was clothes and debris as high as the windows in the back seat and passenger side of the car. Now I'll admit this guy isn't the sharpest tool in the shed, but he's ok, a little weird maybe, but all in all an OK fella.

A few weeks earlier we had installed a new ignition module in it, and it was about as much as he could afford. He really had a hard time handing over that check for the repair. He even made the comment "I hope I don't have to see you any time soon." It's the usual response I get. You have to charge for what you do, that's why it's called a job. But some people think that once you fix one thing you become responsible for every detail of their car. They forget or don't understand that when a car leaves the protective care of the dealership it is up to you to maintain it. The older the car gets the more likely you will be spending money on it to keep it on the road. Now this particular car was far from being maintained properly. I sometimes wondered how the doors stayed attached to the rest of the car.

I was in for an ear full from this guy on the phone. Seems he was about 130 miles away, and the car just suddenly died. He was not happy at all.

I told him, "Calm down, sir. Let's get the car back to the shop, and see what's wrong with it. Unless you know someone down there who can look at it." I said.

"No I don't." he said, "Besides, you're the last person to work on it, so I know it something you did." (Profanity left out).

I had to hold my tongue on this one.

At this point I don't have a clue what's wrong with it, so how in the world does this rocket scientist have it entirely figured out.

I told him that if it was something I did I would be glad to pay for the tow and repair. However, if it's not, it would be on him.

"Oh, you know you'll say it was something else, just so I'll have to pay for it." He replied.

"Ok then," I said, "You ride up with the tow truck, and be here with it when I look at the car. That way we'll both find out together." Several hours later the tow truck showed up with the genius in the passenger seat.

A common practice with roll back tow trucks is to tilt the bed and then let the car out of park, so that the tow cable can then ease the car back on to terra firma. In this case I was standing right there, and I offered to help the tow driver by climbing up there and taking it out of gear for him. Since I was in the driver seat already with my foot on the brake it might be a good time to try and start it. I turned the key, and the old Ford started right up. We let it back on the ground and I left it running. I turned to our illustrious know it all. "Well, now what? I said, seems to be running just fine now." He didn't have a thought in his head at this point.

The tow driver had that look on his face as if to say, "I put up with this guy for 3 hours in the truck....don't make me put it back. I just want to get paid and get out of here." Now it was the car's turn... zoom, zoom, clatter, clatter, hick-up, clunk. Oh shit, it died. Here we go. Now the owner starts in on me.

"Hold on, hold on sir," I was quick to answer. "Let's see what the problem is first."

While the tow driver was re-leveling his bed I was busy checking out the car. I began to think out load, "Now what would make a car start on an angle but die when horizontal? It's like you were parking your car on a steep driveway. Oh crap....check the gas gauge......yep......EMPTY. It was out of gas. Before the tow driver had time to pull around front and collect on his big tow of the day, I put a few gallons in the tank, and had the car running like a champ. It was now showing 1/8 of a tank.

I told the tool shed graduate, "Go up front and pay the man, because it's not my fault you can't watch how much gas you have in the car. You did this to yourself."

You know, this cracker jack of wisdom has been back to my shop many times since then, but he has never apologized for what he said to me that day. I consider it a just reward. Have your car towed 130 miles for a gallon or two of gasoline, and see if you are a happy camper.

I guess you wouldn't want anybody else to know. Except for me....

NO REVERSE

When a new customer comes in the door you sometimes feel that you need to be on guard against any kind of verbal diagnosis they may take the wrong way. You try to carefully answer their questions, and make sure to cover all the related problems that may be associated with what brought them to your door in the first place. It's not like you are trying to be unresponsive to their questions, but you are just trying to make sure you don't say the wrong thing, and they see it as you are unsure of the problem they are having.

On the other hand, you need to be on guard against the unknown customer who has a chip on his shoulder over the last mechanic they have been too. You can tell; they have that look of a secret service agent entering a room and are extremely cautious with any information regarding their vehicle. Or, there is something they are hiding, something you (the mechanic) should be aware of before you even start the repair. It's one of those things that can catch you off guard when you start this new job. This was one of those jobs.

This guy came in with late 70's Chevelle. The turn signals didn't work and that's all he wanted me to look at. The car was outside the front door facing the office, and wasn't in that bad of shape. It was definitely a good candidate for restoring. The owner seemed very edgy; very angry at the whole situation. Not angry, as in "mad at the world", but angry in the fact that he had to bring his car to someone else to fix it. At least that's what I thought. For all I knew he was just the kind of character who just gave the whole world a bitter outlook.

He had a ride home, and left me his number to call him back when I had an estimate. When I went out to the car and started it up, there was one thing that was very apparent. It had no reverse. None, zilch, nada, not happening. Everything else worked fine, just the reverse was not working. Since it was pulled up to the door facing the office it was apparent to me that he must know about this, at least I thought so. I got out, and gave it a push back far enough to allow me to put it in drive and get it into the shop.

The turn signal problem was straight forward, nothing really hard to repair, just a new turn signal switch. I got the job approved, and installed it later that day. While I had it in the shop I thought I would kill some time and see if I could find out what was wrong with the reverse. I looked underneath to make sure all the linkage was intact. It was. I even tried to manually putting it in reverse. Nothing doing. It was definitely an internal problem. Oh well, since I had to "back" out of the shop it seemed the most likely thing to just push it out and leave it on the far side of the parking lot, facing forward. I thought I was doing a good deed, helping the guy out.

That afternoon the grumpy customer showed up to pick up the car. He came in and paid for the job, and walked out without even a thank you. I kept my eye on the guy, not to be nosey, but to see what he was going to do. The way it was parked he didn't need to put it in reverse just drop it in drive and pull forward. If he would put it in reverse he would have had to go over the sidewalk and down the curb onto the street. It just didn't seem logical to even attempt to put it in reverse. As I watched out the window I could see him place the shifter down to the reverse position and then slam it back into park. Out of the car he came with an even louder slam of the driver's door. You could tell this guy was up to something. He started marching right to the office door. I waited for him to open the door, and then said to him, "I already know it doesn't have reverse. I took a look at it for you. It's an internal transmission problem. I can recommend a place for that repair if you like."

He didn't say a word, his whole expression changed from an angry snarl to a look of "DAMN, he knows". Without saying another word he walked back to his car and drove off. If it was a chess match, it's game over fella, check mate.

I never saw the guy again, and I don't know what he ever did with his transmission problem, or whether or not he tried the same trick at the next repair shop. Well I hope his turn signals are still working, but if I were him, I would work on a better opening strategy for his next game.

I'VE GOT A PROBLEM—
I DIDN'T GET
YOUR PROBLEM

This has happened so many times, I've lost track of them all. You have a customer come to the shop and they tell you just enough information to let you assume you can make the repair, but not enough to give a good description of the extent of the problem.

It's not that they avoid telling you the whole story, they just don't think it's important. Even when you try to ask questions about what's wrong, they are short and not very clear on the exact problem. Or they feel they are intelligent enough to figure out the solution to their problem, and all they need from you is one little tidbit of information.

On the other hand, some of them go into such great detail and go on and on with their fatal demise of their beloved ride that you start to wonder....which is really the problem....the car or the driver. What seems to hold true more times than not is one of my old sayings. "If the story is long, the problem is small, and if the story is short, it's going to be a big problem".

MY CAR, IT WON'T SHUT OFF!

A mid 80's Oldsmobile with a diesel engine in it arrived one morning at the shop. The lady who owned it had a very interesting story to tell. It wouldn't shut off. The only way she knew how to get the thing to die was turn on the left or right turn signal. Her car had been at several repair shops, and no one could narrow down what was causing her unusual problem. It was definitely a challenge for sure.

As it always seems to work out this way, a short to the point answer to the question, "What's wrong with your car?" wasn't enough. This generally means it's not going to be a simple fix. I think it's out of shear frustration that the customer doesn't feel the need to tell certain facts. They want the car fixed, and you're supposed to be the expert. Figure it out.

Now you don't have to go into "Dog Story" detail, and I don't need to know what the last shop has tried in detail, (unless asked). But some details can be very important. Take for example: How long has it been like this? When did it start acting like this? Was the problem noticed after any other repairs were done? This kind of information can help lead to a quicker diagnosis of the problem. What the last shop tried may need to be rechecked to make sure it's not masking another problem, or for that matter something may not have been done correctly to begin with. Making the same mistake over and over again is still a mistake. Solving a problem is getting rid of mistakes. And that's what I was going to try to do for this lady.

First things first, I turned the key and waited for the glow plugs to warm up. I flipped the key into start, and it roared right to life. It sounded like a typical diesel engine clattering away under the hood. Now it was time to see this unusual problem. I turned the key off, the engine stayed running just as she said it would. What now? Well, I guess I'll try the left turn signal. The engine shut off and no signs of a problem. This was true with the right turn signal also, but nothing else would shut the engine off. Any dial, knob, switch you could move wouldn't shut it off. I have to admit the lady had a real strange problem on her hands.

I called the lady back. "Was there anything done electrically to the car? Maybe wired in a trailer, added a stereo, or anything done under the hood I should know about?" I asked her.

"No, nothing out of the ordinary," she replied. Nothing out of the ordinary? I could tell she wasn't going to be much help.

Pouring over the schematics didn't help much either. I knew the answer was on that piece of paper, but it just wasn't jumping out at me. Next thought was where to start. A glance under the hood didn't provide much of a clue, but then again I had this feeling I was staring at the problem but didn't know it. One more call back to the customer. "Can you tell me a little more about when this problem started ma'am?" I asked.

"Oh, I don't know, it could have been on a Thursday or maybe a Friday." She answered.

"Is there anything that happened on that Thursday or Friday that I should know about?" I asked again.

"No I don't think it was on a Thursday. It was a month or so ago." She answered.

This is going nowhere; these curve ball answers aren't helping at all. I had to try a new strategy. "Ma'am, in order to make a diagnosis and repair I may need to take the instrument cluster out and some of the engine compartment wiring to track down the root cause of this problem." I stated back to her in a rather monotone voice.

"Ok." She answered. Geez, talk about lack of communication here.

"Well, ma'am, it may get into additional costs that might make it rather expensive to repair, due to the amount of components that I will need to remove just to trace it out." I said.

"No need to worry, I'll pay for it, I need it fixed." She answered.

With that green light it was off to the races. Taking the instrument cluster out it did proved one thing. The cause of the problem was related to the dash in some way. If I disconnected the dash the engine wouldn't shut off at all. Even the turn signals wouldn't kill it. I had to plug the dash back in to get it back to the way it was originally. Turning the dash over and tracing out the printed circuit board, I could see that the diesel computer had its own hidden alternator indicator light. It's on the schematic, but if you are looking at the dash you can't see it. It's blacked out and totally hidden from view. The hidden indicator ran down to the diesel computer and the diesel computer leads ran out to the engine compartment. The standard alternator/charge light wiring was part of the regular car wiring harness that would have been part of a gas engine vehicle. That wiring harness leaves the dash area and enters the engine compartment on the driver's side of the car. The diesel wiring harness enters the engine bay on the passenger side. But, the charge indicators both end up on the same connector at the alternator, just from different directions. That's when I found it.

Our short on information customer had neglected to tell me that this engine had recently been installed. When the tech pulled the old engine out, he would have put the engine wiring harnesses out of harm's way, one on the driver's side and one on the passenger side. After installing the new engine, the tech started hooking things back up, but he made one critical mistake. The diesel alternator indicator wiring connector looks just like the air conditioning clutch coil connector, except for color they could attach to either place. Both have two wires, and both have flat spade type terminals. For whatever reason, the tech hooked up the alternator connector to the a/c clutch instead of back onto the alternator. The proper a/c clutch coil connector was neatly tucked back into the passenger corner of the wheel well and completely out of sight. (Both the diesel and a/c wiring came out of the passenger side of the firewall.)

With the diesel alternator wiring connector in the wrong place and connected to the coil on the a/c clutch electrical, current had a way to return to the diesel computer by way of its second wire and that's what kept it on. The hidden alternator indicator in the dash received its primary (correct) voltage from the same place the turn signals did. Thus, a back feed was occuring and that's what made it all happen.

She paid the bill and then was very chatty, she said. "I had to hock my wedding ring to get my car out of your shop."

"Wow, I'm sorry about that ma'am." I answered.

"No big deal," she replied. "I did about the same thing to get the new engine put in it. I sold almost all my furniture and other jewelry to get that done." She went on to describe the ring, the furniture, all the other jewelry, etc. Now she wants to tell me all the details.... Go figure.

I'm not sure knowing that the engine had just been changed would have made it any easier or not. But I know one thing, it wouldn't have hurt one bit to have given me more info, even if it was a Thursday or a Friday, or even a month ago.

ALL I WANT TO KNOW

My daughter took a call on a 1982 Camaro. The guy refused to talk to her. He wanted to talk to someone who understood the intricacies of his particular vehicle, and could communicate in an intelligent manner about the inner workings of his electrical system. I guess that's me, so now I get to talk to the intellectual giant. The caller told me he was once in my shop with this same car years and years ago. Since then he has taken the computer out of the car, changed engines, changed to a different carburetor, and he was having a problem he couldn't solve.

"What's your problem now?" I asked.

"It's the spark. The quantified value of voltage is not efficient enough to overcome the resistance of the given impedance value in the primary coil. I have already determined that it's not traveling down the wires to the spark plugs in the prescribed manner," he answered. "It's causing a great deal of carbon particulates to be expelled from the exhaust system. What I need to know is can you tell me how much spark there is."

"Sure." I answered. (Give me a break! Now, I have heard of "know-it-alls" before, but this is just out there on the limb of insanity all by itself.)

"With the way the fuel is being consumed in the cylinders, it's obvious that the detonation of each spark plug has reached its threshold." He replied.

"I guess that's one possibility, but I think you may want to check on a few other things while you're at it." I told him.

"Oh no, I'm sure that's where the problem is." He answered. "I've already looked into the angle of deflection across the spark plug gap, so I know that can't be the problem. Just the primary coil voltage is all I need checked. You can do that, right?" he said.

The angle of deflection? What the hell is that? I think this genius is still wearing his team jacket from the psycho ward.

I guess the appropriate answer would have been yes, and answer only the question he actually asked, (Can you measure the voltage from the coil) but I am a "stickler" for details. Besides I don't get a lot of chances to speak to such a scholar of automotive knowledge. I decided to play along, and see where this ended up. "So what kind of cam are you running? What size carburetor is on the engine? What's the compression like? How about the plugs? Do you have cold or hot running plugs in it? Any vacuum leaks you know of? Intake leaks to carburetor base gaskets can be another source of a problem. Did you check the dynamic timing or do you know where the static timing is set? There are a lot of questions I need answered before I can really help you." I strongly replied to him.

He had no answer to the technical questions I asked him, other than, "I don't know."

You know, it's not that I think I know what's wrong. I don't. But when it comes to getting paid to perform work on a customer's car it would be nice to know that I'm actually helping. The fact is this guy hasn't a clue what he is talking about. At the same time, trying to sound intelligent only tells me he is just jumping around from idea to idea, but never coming up with any solutions other than ones he creates himself.

I haven't a clue if this guy will ever show up. As lost as he sounded, I'm not sure he knows where the shop is. Maybe I'll just move, and he won't find me.

JUST A LITTLE FIRE

One day I get a call from an insurance adjuster telling me he has a car to bring by. He hasn't seen it yet, but he is betting that the lady had her story straight, and that it's just as she described it. A minor bit of fire damage around the instrument cluster, nothing more. It wasn't a "I was driving down the road to grandma's funeral" story. It was just a little fire damage, nothing more to worry about.

Later that afternoon a tow truck arrived with this little pick-up truck in tow. The owner was right behind the tow truck, and watched her truck being unloaded. While this was going on I was in the front office writing up a work order with the name of the insurance company on it. About then the tow driver and the owner came into the office. "It not as bad as it looks, it's just a little dash fire." said the owner to the tow driver. The tow driver gave me that look, you know, the one. The look of "You ain't going to believe this one."

After getting all the proper documents together and phone numbers, the lady thanked me, and headed home to wait for our call. I still haven't gone out to the truck to survey the damage, but I know I should. The tow driver left through the front door just shaking his head. Am I worried, nah, it's an insurance job. They have already got this job ready to go.

Now, I have seen little dash fires in the past, and quite frankly that's what I was expecting. The little lady sounded so convincing, and even had the insurance company man convinced. I was in shock when I saw her version of a "little" dash fire.

The windshield is melted down around what was left of the steering wheel. The instrument cluster was just one large piece of oozing plastic that looked like it was poured over the steering column. For that matter, the steering wheel was down to the steel inner lining and the seat, carpet, headliner were all burnt. I couldn't tell the ignition switch from the emergency brake lever. Everything looked like it was poured out of a volcano. Even the driver's door and outside mirror were scorched with smoke and flames.

Come on now. Is this a little fire...or what? Next call is to the insurance company. "You're not going to believe this one." I told the adjuster.

"Oh, I don't know," he said. "I have probably seen more fires than you have. It can't be all that bad. I'll be over in an hour."

When the adjuster got there and walked out to the car, he just stood there. He stood there and looked, and looked some more. He looked back at me, then at the sky, then back at the car. Once around the car and a couple of quick photos was all he needed. "I'll have the tow company pick up and take it to our lot tomorrow. Sorry about this one." he said.

You could see he got a chuckle out of it. Being duped by a sweet convincing lady, who told him it was just a little dash fire. That'll teach ya. If the story is short be prepared for a big problem.

I KNOW I AM THE ONLY ONE WHO HAS EVER HAD THIS PROBLEM

Now here is a guy who has watched too many infomercials, and spent too much time on the internet searching for results about his poor car's condition. I'll bet he's probably talked to anyone with a wrench in their hand about this car.

As always, if the story is long the problem is small, and this was no exception. He started off with what I thought was a weird way of introducing himself. "Hi, I know I'm the only one you have ever had with this problem. I already know my alternator is going out, and so is my starter." He said. "It's a Saturn, but I don't know what kind." He answered while digging thru his wallet for the insurance card. (You don't know your type of car, but you know the problem? (RED FLAG)) "I was told you have one of those machines." he said to me.

"I have scanners, if that's what you're asking, but tell me what the problem is, without telling me the parts that you believe to be faulty. Then I can determine if a scanner is necessary for your type of problem." I said.

It was pretty obvious that he has been given all kinds of bad information on what's wrong with his car. Most of this information wasn't factual or even close to what was wrong with the car. "I had it checked at the other place." he said. The other place was one of those discount part stores where they will come out to the parking lot, and check your car for you. "Everything just shuts off and the only way to start the car when it does this is to wiggle the shifter back and forth really hard." He said. "It doesn't sound like an alternator or a starter to me. Did you try anything else to see if it would start?" I said to him. "No, nobody ever suggested that before." He said.

"It sounds like a loose connection; probably near the battery would be my guess." I told him.

I already had a pretty good idea what was wrong with the car, but "mister info" had to continue with his details. "It's happening more and more often. I have to reset the clock every time, so I know if you'll put it on the scanner it will show you what needs done." He went on with more and more nonsense information. But, I listened intently as he described the problem in such breath taking detail. I was waiting for him to solve it before he handed me the keys. He came so close, so many times, of saying what the problem was, but then changed the story into some sort of TV science fiction saga. I was waiting for the credits to run, or a narrator to start telling me how long, long ago it all started.

He didn't get that far, though. I told him, "There is no magical scanner that can find this type of problem, at least not that I have heard of." Now there is Mr. Spock's "Tri-quarter" It could solve any problem out there. Why, it could analyze the interior of a space ship, broken bones; it could even analyze compounds of planetary rock formations. (I could use that machine) Or maybe I could call on a couple of witch doctors to run around the car chanting during a full moon. No, they're not available this week. There's got to be something in this universe that can solve this mystery. He's the only one in the world with this problem......can somebody help him?!!!

Later that day I got a chance to check this thing out. I turned the key, click, click, click. I can't believe what I'm hearing, should I jiggle the shifter.....sure why not. It turned over once, then click, click, click. I think I'll check the battery connections. Hmm, aren't you supposed to have both clamps tight on the battery? Hmm, I wonder if Mr. Spock picked this up on his scanner.

Well, it turned out it wasn't space aliens or anti-matter from some unknown planet causing the problem. Not a major malfunction that required a never ending diagnostic or witch doctors and full moons. Just plain old diagnostics and a good understanding of what a customer was really trying to tell me, and not just the fluff from all his "other" sources. One new battery and a new set of battery bolts, and he is back on planet earth. Keep trying, maybe next time, you could be the one and only.

NOTE: Anytime you take your car in for repair, just tell the person behind the counter the symptoms, don't try and fix it, and don't try to make it sound like we need to get Mr. Spock... it's a car, not a space ship. Listen up to the tech, if it doesn't sound right to you, ask again. And this time have him explain the results.

IT JUST DIES

An early 90's Lincoln came in with a simple problem, or I thought it would be simple. All the lady would say is that her cars dies. Nothing more nothing less. Every time I would ask for specifics I would get the standard "I don't know."

Taking the car around the block several times didn't do any good, as it ran fine. I put it in the shop and let it run for several hours. Nothing, not a thing, I was waiting for an ignition failure, fuel problem, overheating problem, anything. I was getting worried that it was going to fall into that hated category of "intermittent". That's one place you just don't want to enter. It's never any good.

Later that day the customer called back "Did you find anything yet?" she asked.

"Nothing ma'am, can you think of anything I should do to make it happen?" I replied.

"Nothing I can think of, but it will die. I guarantee it." She said.

Am I going to get anywhere with this car? I guess I'll go drive it around again. Nothing happened. No problems at all. I'm really getting tired of this. All I'm doing is eating up valuable shop time chasing a ghost problem. This lady just has to have more information for me, or else I'm done with this car.

Back to the shop, and back on the phones again. "Ma'am, tell me about the last time this happened. I need as much detail as you can remember." I pleaded. No dice, she just didn't have the vocabulary to explain about it. All her answers were short and not very informative. I'm not sure if it was the fact that she didn't want to sound stupid, or the fact that she was. Either way I'm on my own. I tried everything to get the information out of her. In desperation I suggested she find some time in her busy day to come down and drive the car for me. I would tag along and see what I could find out. Nope, can't do that either. "Ok then, what part of town were you driving in?

"I don't know"

This is getting frustrating.

Alright then, this is it! I'm going to give it one more try. This time it's not Mr. Nice Guy. It's a full out, rip snort'n, bury the gas pedal, tire shredd'n trip around the block. If I don't find the problem, I'll make a problem. I didn't make it around the first corner when the Town Car died. I dropped it back into neutral and turned the key. It started right back up though. Down to the next corner like an Indy driver, half way thru the next corner....dead again. Restarted it, and off to the next corner. This time I drove like a little old lady the rest of the way around. It never stalled, never even tried to miss. What now, for Pete sake? I wish this lady was here. I had a feeling I knew how she drives her car. I tried the same trip over and over again and the results were the same. At least now I know it's not intermittent. There IS a pattern. There IS a way to solve this.

Putting the car back up on the lift gave me the answer. In the back part of the car the fuel pump wiring leaves the fuel tank and heads up under the back seat area. Before it gets there, the rear torsion bar suspension can also be found in that general area. With enough body twist and enough momentum the wire harness would slightly graze the torsion bar. This was enough to shut down the fuel pump for just a second and that would, of course, shut down the entire engine. Oh you might ask, why didn't it blow a fuse? Another example of not enough information. Seems the last mechanic to try and solve the problem had removed the fuse and replaced it with a breaker. (Breaker's are just like a fuse except it can reset itself without having to be replaced)

After telling the customer the results, everything made sense to her. Seems it only did it when she took all the girls to bowling practice. (Really, ya think you could have mentioned that before?!) So it wasn't exactly her driving style as I originally thought. It was the total weight that was being carried. Five ladies and 5 bowling balls, shoes, purses, and whatever else they brought with them lowered the suspension just enough to make contact with the wire without having to drop the hammer on the old Lincoln, and try to drift it around a corner.

This entire repair may have started with an open frame, but I think it ended in a strike. Keep bowling ladies, I'll keep fixing cars.

FOREIGN AFFAIRS

Diplomatic I'm not. A linguist I'm not. But you do run into situations that you need to be a little of both. Over the years there have been many times I wish I spoke a foreign language, or maybe studied the customs of other cultures before going into business. I'm not surprised when an individual who has a heavy accent has a hard time getting his point across. From the grocer to the policeman there is a never ending struggle dealing with the communication level of someone who doesn't speak the language well.

Even in the repair business I have to deal with the language barrier. I have even had people who couldn't speak at all, and would have to write everything down. After awhile, you can get the message across and you can arrive at the problem at hand. You can almost always see the relief in their faces when they realize you have finally understood what they have been trying to tell you. Sometimes funny, sometimes not so funny, but it makes a great story, none the less.

THE CIRCUS IS IN TOWN

Talk about a language barrier. Two Russian fellas came into the shop with a problem. Between the two of them they only knew a few words of English.

One of them knew a bit of English, a few words put together making up a sentence or two, but that was about all he could do. It was hard enough just figuring out if they knew they were at the right place to get their van fixed. It was another thing to figure out what their car problem was. One of them was holding onto the fuse box lid and pointing at their van and a particular fuse on the fuse box chart.

After much pointing, and gesturing I got the idea it was the parking light circuit that was their problem. All three of us headed out to the van. One problem though, it had a trailer attached to the van. Forget about the trailer....there is a bear in that trailer! A big, black, Russian bear.

They unhooked the trailer and let me take the van into the shop to find the problem. One of the guys came with me and the other stayed with the bear. Thank God for that. I didn't need a bear running around in my business!

The Russian fella who came with me was the one who knew a few words of English. He probably knew little more English than I knew Russian, though. Even with the language barrier we got down to the business of finding the problem. After I showed him the schematics of his van, he was even more intrigued to find the solution to his problems. I'm not sure he could read the print but he did seem to be following along with great care, as if not to miss anything.

After awhile I narrowed down the problem area. It had to be in the back of the vehicle, in the tail section. As I traced the problem closer and closer to the actual bad spot my Russian helper was getting the hang of helping me out. I would tell him the color of the wire in English and he would say it in Russian. I would then say whether it was good or bad, and go onto to the next one.

Pretty soon I found the problem area. It was the trailer hitch. I unbolted part of it from the body of the van, and pulled the flattened wire from between the frame and the new trailer hitch. You could see the excitement in his face, but that soon faded into a determined, angry, "I know who did this" expression. Without a word he sprang to his feet and ran outside.

Now the two were arguing outside. I hadn't a clue what was going on, until he brought his friend into the shop, and pointed at the location of the problem. The guy who was watching the bear this whole time came over, and (I think) apologizes to me in Russian. The whole time his buddy is in the background with his arms folded and nodding his head.

Ok, now I get it. The bear watching dude is the trailer hitch installer. No wonder there was this sincere apology from a guy I didn't even know. It was his friend who was watching me do all the work who put him up to the apology.

We got a free bear show that day, and a couple of great new friends. Once in a great while, when the circus is back in town, the two of them show up at the shop, minus the bear, to say hi. Their English is a whole lot better. My Russian.....not so good.

I ONLY SPEAK ENGLISH

It was the middle of summer, quite busy, and getting hotter. An old Chevy Citation came in for repairs. Not exactly in what you might call "A-1" shape, but none the less, it wasn't that bad.

The owner of this car was definitely not from around here. He had a very distinct accent, probably Australian, or South African. He was a real likeable guy, always joking around. He could stand around and talk for hours, if you let him.

His main problem, as he put it, was his "bloody indicator". I asked, "Does it come on and stay on?"

His answer, "Why, I don't rightly know ol' chap. You can figure that out yourself 'cause I know you're one of those dodgy dodger kind of fellows. (I haven't a clue what he just said.)

As soon as I started it up I could see a problem. His alternator light was glowing brightly. Once I had it in the shop and got the hood propped open, I checked the alternator output. 12volts...not good, should be around 14 volts. Well, then I guess I am one of those dodgy dodger kind of fellow's. I found his bloody indicator problem.

I got the ok to put in a replacement alternator and waited for him to pick it up. As before, he was a talkative gent, as friendly as anyone could be. We were becoming quite good mates, I might add.

Out the door and into his car he went with a whistle and skip in his step. That was until he started it up. Back through the door our new found mate came, with a chip on his shoulder.

"Now, might I have a word with you" he said. I guess this means we ain't friends anymore, or is this just another of his jokes.

We went out to the car so he could show me his problem. I got behind the wheel and started it up. The alternator indicator came on with the key and went off once it started. So what's the big deal? That's when he reached in and moved the turn signal lever. "Ya see mate, the bloody indicator still doesn't work. It just stays there, lit up! Not doing a bloody thing, mind ya. Can ya help me out of this jam, because I believe I'm in a bit of a sticky wicket ya see?" He exclaimed.

I had to keeping from laughing. Oh I thought it was funny, but I didn't think my new mate was going to be laughing. "Well, mate, here's the deal. In America we call these little lights in the dash "indicators," I said. "Not just the turn signals, they are all indicators of one form or another. I'll pull it back into the shop and see what I can do."

Luckily it was only a flasher and nothing more serious. And he did understand about the alternator, by the way. We had a good laugh over what it took to get the message across to each other. But we both learned how much language can affect the outcome of people and their perceptions of one and other. The best part was that I received an education in the "proper" terminology of automobile parts the way the other parts of the world understands them.

So, if you run out of petrol, and throw the can on the bonnet, which then bounces up and breaks the windscreen.........well you're not having a cracker of a day for sure. Cheery O.

I SPEAK AH NO ENGLISH

My wife was in the office one afternoon when a referral came in from one of the larger auto parts supply stores in town. This guy had purchased some fog lamps and wanted them installed as soon as possible. It was a little slow that day, so I didn't have a problem getting directly to it.

The customer stayed in the waiting room, and made small talk with the wife the whole time, while I went out to estimate the cost of the installation. I told my wife what I thought it would take to get them installed. She then turned and told the customer the cost of the repair. He said ok—get it done. They continued their conversation as I went to work. But every time she would mention the cost of the repair his English was worse than the last time.

It went from perfect English to some form of Middle Eastern gibberish. Now instead of small talk, it was a language barrier brought on by this guy's refusal to understand that he was going to be charged for the repair. By the time he understood that the backwards English wasn't going to work, he started pulling out his checkbook. My wife is the easiest going person I have ever met. She loves to quilt and bake cookies, and has a smile for everyone. Easy going is her method. You hardly ever hear her raise her voice. Now I've seen my wife mad. I've seen her angry, but I have never seen her this angry. This guy managed to push the wrong buttons, and it was not going to be a pretty sight in the front office that day.

By the time I was done, it had escalated to a full blown shouting match. Oh brother, what now? That's when the wife told me what was going on. I looked at this guy, and I don't know if he was really thinking these antics were going to work, or he really didn't understand her.

How could you tell? Why, he couldn't speak a word of English by this time. My wife leans over to me whispered in my ear, "Offer him 20 dollars off the cost of the job and watch his English improve."

Alright then, "Ok fella, I'll tell what I'll do, I'll take 20 dollars off of the invoice, how's that?" I said. It's a miracle; my wife has cured this poor man of his loss of coherent understanding of the English language. It's amazing! His check book flopped open and he had that check written out before you could blink.

I didn't want his check, no I didn't. It's not about the money, it's about being honest and up front with your fellow man. I threw his keys at him and told him to get out. "Take your car, and get out. Nobody comes in here and gets my wife this upset over a couple of fog lamps." I said. "Leave mister, right now!"

He left, and went straight back to the place that sent him here in the first place. He told them his side of the story; they called me, and asked me what had happened. When I told them what my side of the story was they had a feeling this guy wasn't telling the whole story. Shortly after that the part store called back and said they had to call the police on this guy. They said that when he was confronted with the story from my side the man became very belligerent, and that he started ranting in some foreign language. I hope this guy doesn't try this act on the police. They may not tell you to get in your car and leave as easily as I did.

I never would have thought this stunt would work. Maybe I should try this at my grocery store or at the mall. I guess it's cheaper when you make people think that you can't understand. Nah, it's not my way of doing business, or treating your fellow man.

MICE

Over the years there have been several of these little critters running through cars. They have chewed wiring right down to the electrical connectors, eaten away at the interiors, and packed away foodstuff in some bizarre places. Crafty little devils, they can get through some of the smallest openings you could ever imagine. When they get into a vehicle they are hard to get rid of. The damage they can do is almost always in the worst possible places. Generally, when a rodent is in your car he will hide in small out of the way places, and start chewing on the wires and insulation. Finding out where they are hiding is hard to do, but getting rid of them can be much harder.

I CAN SEE YOU

A tow-in came to the shop one day. We just call them "D.O.A" (dead on arrival). This one was definitely a mouse problem. All the injector wiring was chewed right down to the connectors. Anything that was plastic was chewed on. All through the engine compartment there were bits and pieces of wiring casings and debris from other rubber hoses. It was going to take some work to get this one back on the road. A decision had to be made whether to pull the old harness out and replace with new, or if it was cost effective to repair what was already there.

The latter was the choice. While getting the engine bay back together, everyone involved, even the owner of the car, missed one small detail.......where's the mouse? Normally when you go through these jobs, you'll find a small nest; or a fluff of fabric that indicates they are about to nest in the car. No such luck this time. I thought I better dig further. The interior of the car looked fine, no sign of a critter—no tracks, none of that "other" trail they normally leave behind. In fact the inside of the car smelled fresh, no hint of you know what. I thought I would just poke around for awhile, and see what I could find. Taking the glove box down didn't add up to much. It looked great to me. But...I better look further. While sitting in the passenger seat, I took my right hand and worked up behind the wiring and duct work of the dash, just trying to feel for anything that's abnormal.

Usually, my general rule of thumb is, that most people who try to do home repairs on the electrical systems in their car will only reach "elbow" deep into the car. It's a good rule of thumb to follow, because as someone is explaining a problem you can get a good idea of how far you will need to go to make the repairs. This isn't a someone... this is a mouse. He doesn't abide by any standard rules.

Hey Look! I Found the Loose Nut!

I reached into the dash area as far as my arm could go. I was better than elbow deep when I felt something that wasn't "factory". Oh, oh, a nest. Crap, this job keeps getting deeper and deeper.

My mind is racing through all the possibilities that I'm going to have to go through to finish this job. But in the mean time...I'm stuck. I've got my hand wedge in there so tight, and my elbow was jammed up against another piece of ducting. It's going to take a bit of wiggle room to get my arm back out. I'm so deep into this dash that I have my chin on the dash and my shoulder in a real awkward position.

Well, you're in this deep, so you might as well try to pull out some of this nest, so you can see what material he was using. Then I can find my next part of the car to tear into.

With my chin stuck to the dash and my arm wedged into the ducting, I could just make out this little furry nose ever so slowly coming up from the defrost duct right in front of me. Holy crap, it's the mouse. I couldn't move....I'M STUCK! The little bugger crawled out and sat right there looking at me. He stared right at me; wiggling his little whiskers, and blinking those beady little black eyes at me. I held my breath and waited for him to move. This little guy just sat there. Then he started moving closer, closer again, and still even closer. This little mouse was practically sitting on my nose. I'm freaking out by now; do I hold my breath longer? Do I try to chase him away with my nose? I can't use my left hand much, as it was what was keeping me propped up.

So, I shouted at the little nose wiggling, wire eating varmint. He wasn't in any hurry to move, but I was. He just casually strolled over to the driver side defrost duct and disappeared out of sight.

I got my hand free and told the customer what had happened. We set some traps in the car and took the interior apart to check for any damage. Luckily we didn't find any.

These days, I don't stick my arm in mouse cars any more. I use a tiny fiber optic camera that will fit into the duct work with no problem. That way I can see the little bugger before he sees me.

THE MOUSE HAS TWO HOUSES

One of my regular customers came in for a routine maintenance schedule. It was one of the easier ones to do, just a couple of filters and an oil change. Get the owner's manual out, and check what needs done depending on the mileage, and pull it up on the computer to make sure it all matched our records.

I opened the trunk to inspect his spare tire, and air it up if needed. I noticed the right rear corner of the spare tire compartment was full of seat cushion stuffing. This is a sure sign he's got a mouse in his car.

I called him, and he was quite shocked, but said he would look into it. A few weeks later, he was back in again. This time it was a starter problem. After he would drive somewhere and leave it sit for about 15 minutes the starter would "click". Sometimes it would take several tries to get the starter to work again.

It was definitely a faulty starter motor on this V8 Lexus. The starter is under the intake manifold. He left the car, and we started on this all day starter change out. Under the intake was not only the starter, but about 20 pounds or more of bird seed.

The starter was almost completely covered with it. I called him back, "Hey, did you ever find that mouse?"

"No, didn't think much of it. Thought you were only kidding," he answered.

"Well, I wasn't," I said. "You better come down here. I'm going to take some pictures of this mess. You're not going to believe it."

He came down, and was shocked at how much bird seed he was carrying around, not to mention how far his car was torn apart. The big question was where did it come from, and where is your little friend? I told him that since this mouse prefers his Lexus, he must be a little on the uptown side. You know, he has his summer pad in the trunk, and his nice warm winter house up here in the engine compartment. What more could a mouse ask for?

I'll bet there is another call to the exterminator coming up.

THE BLOWER JUST QUIT

Here was a little old lady with a mid 90's Cadillac with no blower. It was that time of the year that you really needed to have one, too. Once the car was in a service bay, I noticed the fan was on, but it was muffled and not blowing any air through the car. I pulled the blower motor out of the car. One look at it, and I knew we had a mouse problem.

The entire blower motor casing was full of dog food, and I don't mean a little bit of dog food. My guess was about 30 lbs. of food. That stuff had to come out. I don't remember any engineer designing a heater system that would double as a dog food storage cabinet. I put the car up on the lift and split the casing apart with a pry bar. It showered dog food forever; dog food was raining down none stop. When I wiggled things around more would fall.

The stuff was going under tool boxes and benches; my service guys were crunching this stuff under their feet. There's no telling how long it took the little rodent to collect all of this in there. By the looks of the car the lady didn't drive too much, so it probably sat in the garage most of the time. It was a mess! Once we got every single piece out of the vents and duct work, we then cleaned out the heater and air conditioning housings. The next big problem was the smell. It was a wet, damp, and musty smell. It smelled like something crawled in there and died. It took longer to get rid of the smell than it did to get the dog food out.

We gave the car back to the little old lady, and she was so grateful. Her only comment on the whole thing was she thought little "Skippy" (her dog) was just eating a lot more than he used to.

I called a friend of mine in the exterminating business, and had him pay a visit to the lady's house.

I'm sure "Skippy" wouldn't mind finding his food left in his bowl, instead of in the Cadillac.

BOYFRIEND / GIRLFRIEND

Oh so classic, the girlfriend's car breaks down, she tows it to the shop, she isn't sure the repair shop is doing the job correctly or is trying to over-charge her for the repair, and here comes her savior …. the boyfriend.

Now, it's not likely the boyfriend even has a clue about cars, or what is going on, but you can be damned sure he is going to make himself sound like he does, no matter how stupid he looks in the end. He'll usually throw in some over the top jargon about cars to try and impress his girlfriend, or try to baffle me with his superb knowledge of automotive technology. I don't know about her, but I'm not impressed. Most of the time it will backfire on the boyfriend, usually when I start explaining simple things in big words, or start using a lot of fancy abbreviations for different sensors that he just doesn't grasp.

I try to speak directly to the owner of the vehicle; more importantly to the person who is going to pay the bill. Sometimes the boyfriend will get a little mouthy if he feels he is being deprived of his God given right to talk about cars, even though he hasn't a clue what he is talking about. Other times it's just the opposite, the boyfriend realizes he is out matched, and finds the nearest corner to huddle into until business is done at the counter. But most of the time it's just a train wreck waiting to happen. You just never know how bad it's going to be until it makes it all the way to the crash zone. The variations are endless. I'll try to give you a few examples in these next stories.

THE GRAND MA CAR

This story isn't about a Grandma. No not hardly, this is about a Grand AM. I gave this car the name Grandma after this boyfriend/girlfriend exchange.

One day a regular customer came in, it was a boyfriend/girlfriend combination. She owned a mid 80's Grand Am with a 4 cylinder engine. Nothing fancy or fast, just good reliable transportation. It really never had any problems with it, just some minor turn signal problems, and the usual preventive maintenance that every car could expect to have done from time to time. She was always real easy to work with, and took good care of her car. Now the boyfriend on the other hand was a racing nut. Oh, everything had to go faster and run stronger. Nothing stock was good enough for him. Everything had to be modified, because, we all know, Detroit can't build it righ (Whatever). Maybe this is why he didn't own a car that ran (It always seems that opposites attract... doesn't it?). Well, after many failed attempts by him to have the girlfriend see things his way, she finally broke down and let him do some work on her car. He came by the shop one day with the car and without the girl-friend. Not for repair, just to ask some questions. You know, the typical car geek way of doing things -hood up and stare at the motor. His question was "They make a Grand Am with a V6 in it, don't they?"

I said, "They sure do."

"So a V6 will fit in this, won't it?", he asked.

"Well," I said, "It can but in this model year the V6 is an injected engine, and there is going to be a lot of modifications that will need to be done."

"I can handle that stuff." He said, and off he went. I didn't see him, the girlfriend, or the car for several months.

Sometime later, a tow truck came to the shop. It was the Grand Am. I couldn't believe it! The boyfriend did it. He pulled the little 4 cylinder out and dropped a V6 in it, but he couldn't get it to run. I guess when he said he could handle it, he meant I could handle it. Great, just great. Now I have to deal with this. My bad, I forgot, I'm the mechanic.... he's the idiot. Well, it turned out that he had switched the engine, but nothing else. The fuel system needed changing. The computer and the wiring harness had to match the engine. I guess he thought it was all the same, but it's not even close to being the same. This thing kept getting deeper and deeper. This was going to be the boyfriend's job. He was going to have to go find the parts himself, and bring them to me. It's surprising how soon the smile leaves their face when they are confronted with an angry girlfriend and an ever increasing repair bill.

He was trying to keep things in a happy mood, but that all changed after he brought me the computer harness. It was cut in half at the firewall connection. I asked him why in the world he cut the harness up. His reply was that it made it easier to get out of the car. This cost him one more trip to the bone yard to find a harness that wasn't cut. I think this guy has been making too many left turns on the track and is still dizzy. (A computer harness can consist of more than 100 wires, and I'm not about to splice that many wires if he can find another harness). He did.

By this time the girlfriend has kicked him out. But the car isn't done. Even though I had it running, there were still a lot of details that needed to be taken care of. The most obvious was the wiper motor. It turns out the V6 and 4 cylinder bodies are different in one major aspect—the location of the wiper motor. On the 4 cylinder engine it is in the middle of the firewall, but on the V6 it is near the driver's side of the firewall. Since this was a 4 cylinder original car, there is no mounting area for the wiper motor on the driver's side of the firewall. You're stuck with what you got.

Girlfriend is P.O'd at her former boyfriend for even starting this mess. After all the money she has spent to take her slow, but able little 4 cylinder car and turn it into a super powered V6 rocket, she couldn't drive it in the rain. I had to do something, so I rigged up a one-wiper-arm-wonder for her. Leaving the wiper motor where it could fit, and only attaching one wiper lever arm might just work. I managed to get one larger wiper blade off a BMW. It managed to clear at least 70 percent of the windshield. It wasn't great, but it worked.

If the boyfriend would have left it alone, the little 4 cylinder, slow, "Grand Ma" Grand Am car would have been just the thing to drive on their honeymoon. But it wasn't meant to be.

Needless to say, I think she will think twice before letting her next boyfriend tear into her car. Stick to the professional mechanics, girl. I think you'll find better friends there.

BRING THE MUSCLE

A soft spoken lady was having her daughters' boyfriend's car towed in for some transmission work. I don't really do transmissions at my shop, but this was, what I thought, a friend of a friend type deal. I agreed to take a look at it. It was a mid 80's mustang with a standard transmission. The transmission was shot. Oh, and do I mean shot. I always thought that a stick shift transmission was bullet proof, but this car proved me wrong. There was so much clanking and banging around the inside of this transmission that I seriously thought it was more like a steel bucket that somebody threw a chain into. There was no fixing this transmission. I called for prices at several locations, such as dealers, salvage, aftermarket, and at some of the transmissions shops I have used in the past. The best deal was from the salvage.

I called the lady and told her the price, and how long it was going to be until I had the part in the shop. She said it sounded great, and to go ahead and order the part. In fact, she prepaid for the part and labor, so it would be easier for the boyfriend to pick it up when it was done (she didn't have to do that...but thinking back on it, I'm so glad she did).

It wasn't long after that phone call that I had a chance to talk to the boyfriend directly. What a little, x-box playing, no manners, wet behind the ears little jerk this kid was. If he was my kid I would have given him a thrashing behind the tool shed. Arrogant little cuss, to say the least. This kid went on and on, about how he and his buddy could build it cheaper than I could get one from the salvage, and they would build it to race standards (what the hell is that?), and have it done long before the part I ordered would show up.

"Well, she has already paid for the parts and labor, and the part is on the way. I can't exactly stop the truck or the order, so what is going to happen is going to happen. Sorry." I said to this little snot nosed delinquent.

Oh he was furious, but I could tell the whole thing didn't come down to the price; hell, he wasn't paying for it. It was that "guy thing" when some other "guy" can figure out your problem, and you and your race buddies can't. There is some testosterone that gets filtered into the conversation, and that's when things just go wrong. I told him to go talk to his girlfriend's mom. She was the one and only one I was dealing with. Since he couldn't come down off his macho self image, I wasn't going to deal with him. Besides, the deal was done. Sorry Junior, you're out of the loop.

Little did I know, the boyfriend has more pull than good ol' me. Even though I'm supposed to be the professional here, the little Casanova had the Mom wrapped around his finger. Good God, this is not going to be an in and out of the shop job. To make matters worse, when the transmission showed up, it was the wrong one. Now I have to call her back, and tell her it will be another long wait for the correct one, and that the salvage company wasn't exactly happy about it, because they said I ordered it wrong. Whatever! I told the salvage company I wasn't paying for the wrong one, just get the correct one and you'll get a check. GEEZ, can this get anymore screwed up than it already is? Oh shit, I shouldn't have said that.

Now mom gets involved. Oh not personally; oh no, she sends some dumb ass kid in a suit and tie WITH a briefcase, trying to pass himself off as some sort of lawyer or "bodyguard" for the well being of the family. Can you believe this? All I'm trying to do is order the correct transmission and get it installed and out the door.

The so called "lawyer" kid was probably about a junior in college, probably pre-law. What an idiot. He opens the briefcase like he is looking at something important and starts to discuss how I am going to stand behind my work. What the hell is this guy talking about? Of course I stand behind what I do. Then he wants to know if I can guarantee that the part is the correct one this time, so that there would not be any more delays.

"Look dipstick, I am not the guy at the salvage yard putting it on the truck. When I see the dam thing, I'll know if it's the right one, and not before then". Doesn't he understand that, or is he that thick headed? What a jerk. This job has gone from a simple install to an all out assault on my personnel abilities and standards of practice. This little wanna-be lawyer kid is acting like he is the judge and jury. I couldn't help but laugh at this tall lanky kid trying to act like some hot shot lawyer with all the correct answers. He kept tripping over his own two big feet, asking stupid questions that didn't even have anything to do with the job. Things like, which tools would I be using, am I using safety jacks, and do I follow the clean air act. I'm not sure, but I don't think it matters much if I use a Snap-On ratchet with a Craftsman socket but he seems to think so. His questions just got to the point of being ludicrous and complete nonsense. After a while I didn't know whether to keep laughing at this complete idiot, or just walk away.

I did everything except say, "Get the hell out!", because the "mom" has already paid for the job, and I'm locked into this until it's done. The salvage yard is locked into this whole thing too, because they had to buy the transmission from another salvage company out of state. Everyone involved is waiting on the correct part and the job to be completed. I would hope that everyone involved is going to "stand behind" what they do. Maybe I should send "lawyer boy" to them. Geez, what a day.

Luckily, the correct transmission came in the next day. I got it installed and checked out; everything was fine with it. I called the mom for the last time. "Your car is ready. I'll have it out front, ready for pickup." I told her.

"Is there a warranty?" she asked.

"Yes, of course there is." I replied.

That was the last time I talked to anyone about this car. I even took a copy of the invoice and thumb tacked it to the wall, so that on the day the warranty was up I was going to rip it to shreds. I did............ and it felt sooooo good.

CUSTOMER
KNOWS BEST

When it comes to letting the customer decide on the repair or the parts, you most certainly are going to end up in a heated discussion. It is either the cost of the repair, the diagnosis of the repair, or what they think needs to be done verses what really needs done. Sometimes they do have it right. Sometimes the part they bring is the correct part for the job. But more often, it's entirely wrong.

What you don't want to happen is the part they bring being the center of attention, and not the task at hand. Meaning, make the repair not cause a new problem with the wrong part.

You'll see what I mean. Read on and you'll get the idea.

I SAID! I WANT THIS WIPER MOTOR INSTALLED!

One day a fella came in the door with a brand new wiper motor under his arm. With a great deal of force and a shoulder high drop to the counter, he body slams the wiper motor to the counter. With no hesitation or a hello, or my name is....He just started ranting "I want this thing installed, and I don't want No for an answer."

"Ok no problem," I said. I was definitely on guard for this one. Something didn't sound right. I thought I'd better play it cool with this guy. So I said "Ah....it will be 45 dollars up front though. This is not the way I normally do business, sir. Normally we diagnose the problem and then go into the repair phase, but if all you want me to do is put that motor in the car, I'll be glad to do it."

He ranted back. "There ain't going to be any of that diagnosing crap. I don't need anybody to tell me how to fix a car. I want it put in, and I want a receipt showing that you guys installed it....and that's that."

Now he is looking at the motor, out the window, looking down at his shoes, everywhere except at me. He begins to rant on and on. "That damned parts store keeps telling me there's nothing wrong with the wiper motor, and that the only way they are going to give me my money back or another replacement one is if I have a shop install it, so they know I ain't doing it wrong. What a crock, having to pay somebody else to put on something that I can damn sure do myself! The nerve of them. Who the hell do they think they are anyway? Damned dumb ass parts counter jockeys. Well I'm here…(he finally looks at me).. get it done"

"Ok, sir, there is the matter of the 45 dollars". He hands me the money. "Thank you. I'll get that motor put on right now".

I installed the motor, never turning it on, and parked it back outside.

A moment later, "What the hell is going on? My wipers are still not working. What the hell did you do wrong? You're just like that parts store. Are you guys working together or what?"

"No sir, we are not working together. Obviously the motor is not your problem. We need to diagnose the problem." I answered.

Now with even more profanity, and even louder he said, "I'll bet that is going to cost me more?"

"Ah ,yes, it will." I answered.

"Not a chance fella. You had your chance to fix it. I'm out of here. Just consider yourself lucky you got that 45 dollars out of me. You can bet I'll never recommend this shop to any of my friends," he said, while he was slamming the front door as hard as he could.

He left, burning rubber all the way out of the parking lot. I'm a so grateful for his last comment. Just think I might have to deal with someone who is friends with this guy. Wow…I'm feeling lucky today……

THE KEY TO THE PROBLEM

I had a late model Nissan come into the shop one summer day. It didn't have an unusual problem, but it was more of an annoyance that was making the owner quite upset. It was the customer's dear wife's car. Seemed almost all the time the steering wheel locked, so she couldn't turn the key to start the car. She would jiggle and wiggle the wheel until she finally got the key to turn, and could go on her merry way. The husband was the one who dropped the car off, and explained the problem to me. I got his phone number and the key, and told him I would call him later with the results.

Now then, the problem. What problem? I couldn't find a problem. I tried and tried to lock the wheel into a position that would make it tough to turn the key, but I couldn't duplicate what he had told me. I even tried parking it outside and putting the wheels against a curb, and turning the wheel. Nothing worked; it just wasn't acting up for me. I had to call him back and tell him. I knew he wasn't going to like it, but I explained to him that I would have to see it acting up to really know what to do with it.

Several days later the same car was back with the same problem. Again I went through every scenario I could think of, and still couldn't find anything. The husband kept insisting it had to have something to do with the steering wheel lock. I didn't agree, but he was insistent. I told him that if he wanted to I could remove the lock tab on the ignition switch, and that way the steering wheel would never lock again. As frustrated as he was with the car, and not seeing anything else to do, he agreed to have that done.

This era of Nissans had an odd way in which the ignition switch was attached to the steering column. This was before we had such sophisticated alarm systems and fancy "proximity" keys. The ignition switch was held on to the steering shaft with two break away bolts that have to be chiseled off to remove the switch. Once I had the switch removed I took it over to the grinder and completely removed the locking pin. I ground that sucker off flat. Now the steering wheel couldn't lock at all, no matter how hard she had it against a curb. It just couldn't be done. Like before, I tried everything I could to make it act up. Same as before, it worked without fail.

Later the next day the husband and his wife came in and paid for the work, and were so happy to finally have this problem behind them. They both told me how proud they were to find someone who would stick with the problem to the very end, and get the situation solved to their satisfaction. I had a smile on my face. I'm not sure why, but it was all sounding pretty good. But then again, I never found the "exact" problem. All I did was take out the lock tab, and stop the steering wheel from locking. Anyway, they went arm and arm out the door both with a smile, and almost dancing to their cars.

As I stared out the front windows of the lobby, I could tell it was taking way to long for her to start her car. Then the husband got out of his car and was throwing both arms in the air, while she sat there with the driver's door open. Oh, oh, they're coming back in....... I better rush out there. I met them half way across the parking lot. "Is there something wrong?" I asked.

"You know damned well there is!" he shouted back at me.

"It's doing the same thing as before," the tearful wife told me.

Now it was my turn to try it. The key wouldn't turn. The steering wasn't locked, it couldn't lock, but that key wasn't budging an inch. I pulled the key out of the ignition, and looked at the key. Hey, this isn't the key I had been using the whole time. "Oh, you've got the wrong key," I told the couple.

No, it was the right key alright. It was the wife's key. The husband had been giving me HIS spare key the whole time. The key she was using had absolutely no teeth left on it. It was almost completely flat and void of any ridges.

"I think your whole entire problem was your key was worn out sir," I told the couple. I tried the key that the husband had originally given me, and it worked flawlessly. The couple just stood there with their chins dropped to the ground.

She was so apologetic. He was in shock. She grabbed his key, and was as happy as she could be. The husband, well, he just stood there like a statue. I think he finally realized that he just spent all this money on a faulty key. "Honey, I guess I need a new spare key, and I'll see you at the house," he very soberly told his wife. He looked at me and nodded, walked to his car and left.

I was the last one standing in the parking lot, and now my chin was on the ground. To think, all this work I had done on this car, only to find out in the end that it had nothing to do with what the customer had originally thought. This definitely called for a cold one after work.

To this day if I get into a situation like this I always look at the key first, and then at the customer. Even if they don't want to give up that spare key I want to see it. The key to solving any problem is having all the correct information.

Even if the solution to the problem, is the key.

ALL MY LIGHTS

A little old lady brought in a 2001 Chevy van. When I asked her what the problem was her only response was that all her lights would blink on and off. "Which lights are you referring to ma'am?" I asked.

"All of them," she replied.

"All of them?" I asked again. "Really? Ok, let me pull it in the shop, and take a look at them."

As I was pulling it in, I could see already it wasn't all the lights, but rather the turn signal indicators were both on whenever I applied the brake pedal. Now I've seen this before on these models; it's a simple matter of replacing the rear light sockets with new "improved" ones with new connectors. (The wiring connection is very small, and generates a lot of heat on the ground connection, thus heating up the connector to the point of failure). So the repair is straight forward, but the preciseness of the customer's response needed to be put into question. With her only comment being that "all" the lights were blinking, and not just the turn signal indicators, I needed to clarify what she actually meant. For that matter the turn signal indicators were not really blinking, but merely coming on when the brake pedal was pushed. I could see where the parking lights would be effected by this condition, and that any stray electrical signal could cause other "lights" to go on and off, but the fact that she said "all" the lights led me to another discussion with the owner, before I made any repairs.

It was like talking to a broken record.....on and on, she would only tell me about all the lights, and didn't understand what I was telling her. I went through the whole entire process of how I brought the van into the shop and what I actually found, and that the repair I was suggesting would take care of what I could see as the problem. This communication was going nowhere. She had to tell me the whole story in her own words, right down to the details of her latest episode with her hair appointment (another dog story no doubt). Now that she had told me (for the third time) what she saw as the problem, and what she could see as a way to repair it, she let me explain (for the third time) what was needed for the actual repairs. Afterwards, she gave me the ok to replace the rear sockets and see if that fixed "all" her lights. I made the repairs, and took the car around the block to verify that everything was working, and that there were no strange lights coming on while I was driving it.

Everything worked great, I couldn't see anything else wrong at this point. Her only comment was whether or not the clock was going to dim anymore. At this point in my life I just can't get excited over trivial things like the light in a clock, but she was a little concerned with it so, like the idiot I am.... I went out and looked at the clock. The only reason she was seeing the clock dim was the fact that the clock is also connected to the dash light controls, which is connected to the park light switch. It was getting a feedback current whenever the brake pedal was pushed, and sending the current back up the park light wiring and through the dash light circuit, and finally to the clock light. It was dimming down, because the day time brightness is different that the night time brightness. Geez, that wore me out explaining that one. Sometimes it feels like the simple explanation is hard to put into layman terms without sounding so technical. Then sometimes the explanation is so technical sounding that they just stare at you, as if they "really" understand but don't, and then assume you must be right because it sounds so technical. Maybe I should have I just said that all the lights are fine ma'am, and left the technical stuff out of the conversation. Just think of all the chatter and gossip that could have been stirred up at the local beauty salon.

CHEETOS ARE CRUNCHY

This is an unusual story to say the least. I had this customer come in with a '79 Cadillac. Not much you can say about a 79, except for the fact that this is one of the first year that a full electronic computer vehicle was produced in main line production in the U.S. It was a crude system, even for those days, but it did work. However, there is no diagnostic hook up for a scanner. No, not even a way to make the check engine light blink a code. The only repair possible, by book standards, was to use a system diagnostics that gave you the values of each electronic component. Not that easy to do when even then the word TPS (throttle position sensor) was completely new to the terminology of automotive repair. So a lot of trial and error methods were developed in the independent industry. Unfortunately this just usually lead to the "let's just swap parts and see what it does" repair method. What a joke. I won't even begin to go into what I think of that method. Geez.....

Well, this Caddy was blowing black smoke out of the tail pipe like there was no tomorrow. All the sensors were in range, and the most likely culprit was the injectors. The car had roughly 100K miles on it, so it seem pretty likely. Although this was 1989, and the car being 10 years old, there wasn't exactly many parts around. The dealer still had replacement injectors, but they were quite expensive. I pulled a few out, and sure enough they were leaking fuel. Not a good sign.

CUSTOMER KNOWS BEST

I told the customer the results of the testing, and he opted to get his own injectors. Bad mistake. The parts he brought to me were out of a junk yard car. God only knows how many trips around the planet this thing had on it. I informed him that he was on his own with used parts. I would only install the parts, and not warranty any work due to the fact that I'm sure that these used parts are not any better than what I was taken out. He said he understood and was willing to take the risk.

I installed the parts. Well, you guessed it......it ran just as bad, if not worse than it did. He was out of money by this time. Totally pissed by now, as if I hadn't warned him about the possibility of what the outcome could be. He was furious. I informed him again of what I told him earlier about using used parts. He paid the bill, and was waiting on a tow truck to haul his poor old Caddy home.

We had a snack box in the waiting room. You know, so customer could grab a little something while waiting. It was on the honor system. No fancy machine, just a box and a slot for the change. Hell, half the time I had to throw in 10 or 20 bucks monthly, because somebody didn't pay up. But this fella did. He grabbed a bag of Cheetos, and sat down to wait for the tow truck. The whole time he was sitting there you could see the gears turning in his head. He would start a conversation with the empty chair next to him and then get quiet while munching on his Cheetos. A few minutes would pass by, and the same thing would happen again.

As the tow truck arrived and was loading up his car, the old Caddy owner was outside yelling at the tow driver and pointing in my direction. The tow driver was being as sympathetic as possible, but this poor Caddy owner had made up his mind that it was time to show me what he thought of the whole thing. He was staring in the window of the lobby to the waiting room area. Glaring, eye brows down, angrily looking at me, he wanted to be sure I was watching. He took his bag of Cheetos, and one by one threw each individual piece on the ground. Then he crushed them with his foot, using a side to side motion, while at the same time holding a dead stare right at me. He was mumbling something of course, and glaring at me, as if to say, if you were a Cheetos this is what I would do to you.

After the tow truck left I grabbed a broom and cleaned up the Cheetos from the front of the shop. What waste of a good Cheetos.

This is the job that led to the term "roping a steer." Whenever a customer would bring his own parts for me to install on their car I would tell them this: If you bring your own parts it was like roping a steer. As soon as I put the part on and tightened the last bolt, I throw my hands in the air and call time. That's it. My job is done. I have already diagnosed it, and now the repair is up to the quality of the replacement parts, which means...you're on your own. If I have done my job right and diagnosed it correctly, there shouldn't be any doubt as to what needs done. However, used parts (especially electrical ones) and/or substandard (cheap) parts tend to have a higher failure rate than good quality parts. It normally ends up back in the shop, retesting for the same problem just to verify that the replacement part is the cause.

It's a whole lot easier if you let the shop assume the entire responsibility, but you have to make sure that it's diagnosed correctly from the start or everything is going to be wrong.

YOU'RE A MECHANIC, RIGHT?

Never fails, at a Christmas party, football game, somewhere other than at the shop, you'll find two guys who are going to start talking cars. Over the years I just bite my lip, and not say a thing. Especially if someone asks me what I do for a living. That's when I try to navigate towards a different end of the buffet table .

Somebody will mention something about a certain problem, and I'll give them the most likely repair. Then some wrench jockey half drunk will put his two cents in, and tell me that I'm full of it. Whatever dude. I would prefer not to answer any questions at parties or at a get together. I don't go to parties and start telling you how to do your profession, so ease up fellas. If you are asking me what I do for small talk, or want to talk cars in an entertaining manner, I'll be glad to sit and chat for hours. If it's going to be a question of do I know more than you...I'm not interested. So I pretty much know now what I should do at parties .... just keep my big mouth shut.

I was at a Christmas party when 2 guys behind me were having a conversation about their cars. Guy #1 was talking about how he has to add water, oil, and other fluids to his ten year old car each month. Guy #2 was agreeing with him, because he had to do the same with his car.

So far so good, then it led into, "it's because they are old, and there is nothing you can do about it. Those new cars cost so much, it just isn't worth it to drop that much on a car. I'll just drive mine until the wheels fall off", said Guy #1.

(I'm really not listening in...seriously I'm not). As the conversation went on, I could see what it was all about....it's male ego. You know... "I know more about cars than you do". Until one of them gives up, the conversation can go on all night. It reminds me of two rams on a hill, bashing their heads together until both the knuckleheads realize that this really hurts. Then they just stand there, each wondering what to say next. On and on these guys went, getting more techy as the night dragged on.

Guy #2, taps me on the shoulder, "Say fella, what do you do for a living?"

Damnit, I already had 2 glasses of wine. Do you think I did the smart thing? Nope. "I'm an automotive tech. I specialize in electronics, but my shop does pretty much any kind of mechanical repair," I said. (I wish I could take that back, I should have said something political...that would have been a hoot.)

"Oh, so you're a mechanic right?" Guy #1 asks. "What do you think of these new cars?"

"They're great, better engineering than before, better fuel economy, performance, style, you name it. I think they're great," I answered back. You would have thought I just spilled their beer or something. You could see these two guys raise their horns for a ramming shot.

"They are not engineered better, what the hell do you know?" Guy #1 said.

"Yeah, you can't beat a 69 body style for looks." Guy #2 blurts out.

"You're right guys, that's why they keep making new and different models. Everyone has their own taste in cars and styles. I think the muscle car era cars have a look all their own. They're nice too," I replied, trying to come up with a way to end it, before reaching ramming speed.

"So what can you tell me about my water leaking out of my Vortec?" asked Guy #1.

"The number one thing I have seen the most of is the intake gasket or the heater hose fitting in the intake." I unfortunately answered, wishing I hadn't.

"Oh, that's bull," Said Guy #2. "My Vortec has never leaked, and I've got about 150 thousand on it."

I had to bite my tongue again. "Mr. Maintenance" is so well informed you know. (Usually what keeps them from not leaking after that many miles is the corrosion built up around the fittings.) Even though I have never looked under this guy's hood, I'll bet it's just covered in massive amounts of crusty oxidized gunk all over the edge of the intake. (Like I said before, don't diagnose without actually looking at the problem.)

"You're probably right, I must be mistaken then." I calmly answered back. After that I found another corner of the buffet. Hopefully one talking about football, golf, quilting or anything but cars!

I JUST CHANGED THAT PART

This was one time I didn't listen to my own advice about doing something for free. I still ended up with a customer, who was not very happy.

It was a little Subaru, well kept, clean, and not a scratch on it. This gentleman agreed to pay for the diagnostics to find out why his battery started to go dead over night.

I ran a draw test on the electrical system. It's a very simple procedure for this year vehicle. Just hook up a test light and start disconnecting circuits until the test light goes out. You can't get much simpler than that. When I raised the hood on this cherry little Subaru I saw there was one new part on the car. The voltage regulator, not a big concern for now, I was still testing the other electrical systems. I soon found out that if I pulled the fuel pump fuse the draw would disappear.

Going back to the prints provided the final clue to this mystery. It's that new voltage regulator. Seems Subaru ran the fuel pump circuit through the regulator on this year's model. I guess the thought was if it stopped charging the battery you should stop the fuel pump. (Weird way of doing it, but I'm not the engineer.)

I put the fuse for the fuel pump back in, and then unplugged that new voltage regulator. The draw was completely gone. There was no doubt about the location of the drain, or what was causing it. It wasn't like it was a highly detailed circuit with hundreds of loop holes that a trace bit of current could have leaked out into the electrical system. It was 110% the problem. The regulator had that look of one of those cheap parts that I tend to shy away from. But I didn't buy it, he did.

I went into the waiting room and told the customer what I found, and that the reason for the battery going dead overnight was because the fuel pump was staying on. To fix it we needed to replace the voltage regulator. "I just put that on. That ain't the problem," he said in a fit of rage.

"Well, it is sir. You see the fuel pump uses that relay as its own fuel pump relay," I told him.

"Oh come on, you don't expect me to buy that hog wash, do ya?" he answered. "You better tell me something other than that. I don't believe you, so why don't you tell me what's really wrong with it. I'm not about to buy your story."

I got the schematics out and showed him how it worked, and how it was really his actual problem. Even then, no dice, he wasn't going to believe it. He refused to pay for the work I had done. He demanded that I give his car back to him, so he could go home and fix it himself.

I didn't want to do that. It seemed a little stupid to give a guy the answer to his problem, then have him call you a liar right to your face, and he still wanted to go home and fix it himself? Geez, what do ya do? I gave in, pulled his cream puff Subaru out of the shop. That's the last I saw of him.

Sometime later, my wife and I were out at a restaurant having a quiet dinner for two. My wife noticed that over at the next table the restaurant manager seemed to be spending a lot of time with this couple. He was kneeling down taking notes, and doing a lot of that "I'm sorry for all the inconvenience" nods and jesters. Shortly after that the couple left their table. By the way, they finished their entire meal, including mixed drinks.

The table directly across from us saw the whole thing too. I looked at that guy and I shrugged my shoulders as if to say, "I don't know". He leaned over, and told me that he was pretty sure the other couple had just taken the restaurant for two dinners and drinks.

The manager came by, and saw us talking. He told us pretty much the same thing. You know it would be different if the meal was terrible, and you left it on the plate. Or the drinks were too strong, and you couldn't finish them. But to eat and drink the whole thing and then complain? Sounds just like the little well kept Subaru guy struck again.

Sometimes you can't please people no matter what you do.

TWISTED HORN

For many years it was common for a customer to bring in a set of aftermarket horns they wanted installed. I never thought the factory horn was all that bad, but some people just wanted to stand out in a traffic jam, or something. Some would go with the multi-play versions and others wanted that robust sound of a tractor-trailer rig.

This guy wanted the old fashion "A-OOGAH" sound on his late 80's Chevy pickup. I was more than eager to help, why not, it's an easy install, and the guy made it even easier. He wanted it to work off his factory horn button. It was a simple project. Open the hood, find the factory horn and disconnect it. Mount a small air compressor to run the new horns, and use the exciting lead that fed the original horn. Find a spot to mount this contraption, and give it a try. It worked perfectly. I didn't think he needed such a thing, but what do I know, I'm just installing it.

One of the guys in the shop pulled it outside, while I handled the transaction at the desk. By the time we had settled up, my helper was walking back in with the owner's keys. We all said our "thank yous" , and he headed out the door, while we all headed back to the shop to work on other projects.

CUSTOMER KNOWS BEST

Looking out in the parking lot there was a strange thing going on. The owner of the vehicle had the hood open and was checking our work. Then he started motioning for someone to come out there. I guess that means me. Geez, what happened now? Did something fall off between the shop and the parking lot? By the time I got to this guy he was steaming, cursing me, and having a fit. "You S.O.Bs, you put my steering wheel on crooked!" he yelled back at me. "Now, by God, you are going to fix this!" he kept ranting at me.

The funny thing is I don't recall taking the steering wheel off. How can this be a major setback to installing a horn under the hood? That's about the time my helper showed up. He grabbed the keys from the guy, and reached in and unlocked the steering wheel, turned the steering wheel straight and handed the customer his keys back. "There ya go, mister," he told him, "I just parked the car with the steering wheel turned a bit. It's fine now." My helper just rolled his eyes at me and didn't want any part of the ranting fit this guy was having.

The guy looked at me, he didn't know what to say. I knew what he wanted to say, but I think he was too embarrassed say it out loud.

"Thanks for coming, I hope we can do something for you in the future." I said with a smile. He never looked back. He just got in his truck and sped off. He was quite a ways down the road when I heard that "A-OOGAH" one last time. I just hope he hasn't tried to park his truck with the steering wheel crooked again. I would hate to have to send the help out to twist his steering wheel straight for him one more time.

YOU'RE JUST A JACKASS

One thing I hate more than anything is when a new customer comes through the shop or the backdoor to start a new job, instead of using the front door. I don't know what it is, but it seems when this happens the job goes wrong. Customers who have known me for years know the boundaries of the shop. They understand that a little respect for the equipment invested in the shop and their personnel safety would go a long way by showing some respect to the shop.

The front door is clearly marked, and there are even signs pointing you in the right direction. In fact, a buzzer on the front door will alert anyone in the back if you enter through the front door. When an unexpected visitor/customer comes in from the rear of the shop this usually indicates a personality trait that is going to be in conflict with mine.

The shop is not a public place; it is a work area, like an emergency room. Sometimes the doctor will let you stay in the room, and sometimes they will tell you to wait outside. It's not just me, I have talked to a lot of shop owners over the years and the story holds true for them, too. Some people feel they have to see the work area to make sure your shop is up to their standards. That's fine, I don't mind, but ask first! As I said before, if a customer comes in the back door, the job will go to hell. It seems it always end up the same way—either the parts aren't available, the job is too expensive, or the customer perceives me as an idiot. Like this little job turned out to be.

The business next door to my shop hired a new secretary. I'd never seen her before, and didn't even know she worked next door until she told me. She pulled alongside the shop and came through the shop overhead doors, and proceeded to go up to the front office by way of the backdoor. I was in the back office where we keep the computer systems with all the schematics, and could see her through the window to the shop.

There was no one up front at the time, as everybody was out to lunch. Customers get a little upset if they have to stand and wait too long, so I got up to the front as quick as I could to help her out. "Can I help you?" I asked.

"Yes, I have a rattle in the front end," she replied. "Can you take a look at it today?"

"Sure can. Leave me the keys, and I'll have somebody look at it after lunch." I answered.

I put the invoice in the new job box, and went back to what I was doing before she came in. A bit later my helper came back and noticed the new job in the box. As you would think he would do, he pulled the car up onto the lift, and started checking it for anything that would make a rattle in the front end.

He called me over a bit later, and said he found 2 problems right off the bat. A broken motor mount and a sway bar end link that was rattling every time you got near it. "I'll call the customer." I said. With that I got the numbers together on the cost of the parts and labor , and gave her a call. She came back with one of those, "You better talk to my husband" answers.

The husband called, and I could already tell this was not a pleasant person at all. He started the conversation with an attitude. I'm not sure, but I think this guy must think every mechanic out there is trying to screw him over. I don't think there was any convincing him of anything different. He wanted to know if I had checked the wheel bearings yet. "That's where the problem is," he said. "I don't know what kind of shop you're running, but you're not going to take advantage of me."

"I'll have the tech check it and I'll call you back." I told him.

Sure enough the driver's side wheel bearing was gone, but so were the other parts too. I called the customer back, and told him he was right on the money about the wheel bearing needing to be replaced. "It's my fault," I said, "the word "rattle" on the invoice should have just been "noise while driving". That way the tech would have checked the entire front end for anything, rather than just what could make a rattle sound."

"You're nothing but a jackass!" he said to me.

"What?" I said with a surprised look.

"If your techs can't find a simple rattle in a car, then I'm not having any work done here." He yells back at me.

"Would you like to see the damage we found sir? The car is still on the lift," I said.

"Nope, I'm taking the car elsewhere." He yelled.

By this time I've had enough of this guy. It's one thing not to check the car as thoroughly as it should have been, but it's a completely disrespectful way of handling things when the guy who is trying to solve the problem is now labeled a jackass. "Ok, then I guess our business is done." I said.

"You're dismissed!" he yells back at me. Now what the hell was that all about?

"No, sir, you're done. Get your car and leave!" I shouted.

"Did you not hear me?" he yells back. "You're dismissed!"

Now I don't know about you, but I got the impression either this was an ex-military guy, or one of those people who just have to get the last word in, no matter if they are right or wrong. Either way, I'm not doing any work for this jerk.

Oh. I still do a lot of work for the rest of the folks next door. I may be a jackass, but I'm a damned good jackass.

CAN YA LOOK AT
MY CAR?

Look folks, I'm in business to make a living, support my family, and buy my kid braces. I am not in the business to give free advice over the phone, or walk out to the parking lot and stare at your car, while you give me your version of the dog story. You want me to fix your car...great. You want free advice.....call one of those radio station talk shows, or get a book and find out what you need to know.

This is one of my pet peeves. This industry is so full of second hand information, and very little apprenticeship programs for younger individuals who would like to get into the trade. It's no wonder things can get screwed up the way they do. If you try to guess at a repair, you're just being foolish. So please, when there is a professional mechanic standing in front of you treat that individual with the same respect you would give any other professional. These next couple of stories are related to this situation.

YOU'RE THE FIRST PERSON I THOUGHT OF

Here's a lady with a turn signal problem. Not a big deal; it's a typical job for me. Her story is that she had gone to a tire shop to have the turn signals looked at. They said it was some sort of electrical problem, and they didn't deal with that kind of problem. She would have to find an electrical shop to have it checked out. Then she called the dealership, and they told her that it's most likely the turn signal switch. So she bought one, and her husband installed it. The turn signals still didn't work. Now she calls me. "Hi, how's it going," she said.

I recognized the voice; it's a gal who did some advertising for me through the local paper. I have probably talked to this lady a hundred times over the past couple of years. I no longer do any advertising, so we kinda lost touch. She told me her problem, and that her husband installed the switch. "Of course you know," she said, "you're the first person I called to look at this problem."

I'm a little confused at this moment. Did I not hear her say it went to a tire shop, and she also made a call to the dealership? "Sounds to me like I am the third person you've contacted about this….not the first!" I said.

"Well, what do you think it is?" she replied. I told her I don't diagnose over the phone, and if I did, I'm probably going to be wrong. When that happens people will buy parts they don't need. Unless they really want to just keep guessing and trying different components, they should bring their car in for diagnosing.

She tried several times to get me to tell her what was wrong with it. She finally decided the best course of action was to bring it in and have me diagnose it. The problem was quite simple. This particular turn signal wiring runs thru a separate hazard flasher switch. The hazard switch was the culprit all along.

No, she didn't want me to fix it, her husband could do that. Even after they paid for the diagnosis I wasn't finished. Hubby now wanted to know how to take the hazard switch out of the dash.

Does it ever end? Maybe I should hold the tools for him too.

I KNOW YOU ALREADY KNOW WHAT'S WRONG

Now I'll admit, if one of my long time customers asked me to step out into parking lot and take a quick glance and their daily driver, I would without hesitation. However, if I don't know you from Adam there isn't much chance you're going to get much more than "let's get it in the shop" from me. This is what happened with a little Ford Probe.

I was eating lunch at my desk, pretty much like I do most every day, when I can find a few minutes to sit down. This guy comes through the shop area and into the back part of the office. Strike ONE. I'm sitting right there, just beyond the back door of the office. I put my sandwich down, and asked him if I could help him.

"Ya sure can partner," he said, "My Probe out here is doing some weird stuff, like the blower fan will work on low and medium, but not on high. And the air conditioning will only come on when I have the fan on high. But ya see, the fan then isn't on. Whatcha think it is, partner?"

I hate to act like a know it all, but I do know exactly what that problem is. "After I have lunch, I'll be glad to get it in the shop and diagnose it for you. Of course, you know that will cost," I said.

"Awe, come on dude," he said, "Sounds like you already know what the problem is. Why would I want to pay for that when you could just tell me what it is, and I can go home and fix it."

I guess I looked like an idiot to this guy, as I was dressed in my finest greasy jacket, sporting an apron of tools, and don't forget those grease stains on the knees of my jeans. I also had all the wiring diagrams strewn in front of me for the job I was just working on, before I decided to have lunch. "Sir, that's how I make a living," I answered back. Here we go again, repeating the same thing over and over again.

He says tell me what's wrong. I say pay me to do it. He repeats his little speech about my knowing what it is already, and I repeat my speech that it's going to cost you. This went on for quite some time. I don't know if I'm as stubborn as a mule (my wife could answer that!), or if it's the principal of the whole thing.

I just can't imagine any profession that routinely gives out free information without a prospect of a financial gain in the long run. With me, if I tell you what the problem is, then there isn't anything left for me do monetarily.

Then again it's like my dad always told me. "You catch more bees with sugar than you do with salt." (I know, it doesn't sound right...but hey, you had to know my dad). It works both ways though. Show me some respect and I will show you some. (I'm eating my lunch for Pete's sake).

I'm also the kinda guy who might see a celebrity in a situation, say like he is at breakfast with his kids, and I'm not going to bother him. Let everybody have their space. Not that I'm some sort of celebrity, but I am a professional at what I do, and I would appreciate a little respect.....at least at lunch time. Well this guy wasn't seeing that side of the coin at all, so it's not likely I'm going to budge from my chair, until I have finished my lunch.

He finally gave up, left the shop with his tires squealing, (that's pretty good for a Probe!), and I went back to my lunch. Oh, I didn't mention what the actual problem was did I? Since, I never really diagnosed it...it would only be a guess. It was......nah, I'll keep that to myself.

IT'S PARKED OUT FRONT

A guy comes into the lobby and looks around at the walls, while waiting on the customer in front of him. He would try to look around corners and through windows to see if there was anyone else that could wait on him. When it's his turn at the counter he asked if there were any techs in the back that might be able to help him. My wife was in the office that day, so she naturally buzzed me to the front.

When I got there I greeted the fella, and asked him if I could help him. He proceeded to tell me about his charging system problem, and how his light bulbs all had to be changed. He mentioned something about the transmission not shifting and that the service lights were on. It all sounded like a problem with the charging system to me, so I told him to talk to the lady at the desk, and she would make an invoice. Then I could start on it. I even told him that it had a hint of being a charging system problem, maybe an alternator or regulator problem, but the best thing would be to have it tested properly.

"Well, can you come outside and just look at it?" he asked. "It's parked out front."

I have a rule about that; I don't like looking at a car in the parking lot. My "office" is in the shop. My tools and equipment are in the shop. The only thing that I can accomplish outside is just a "look", and more times than not I have found that all I end up with is a "thanks a lot", as the guy drives off with his new found knowledge. I make it a rule that if I don't know you, I don't go to the parking lot. You're going to have to be pretty convincing to even get me to poke my head out the door.

I put on my best persuasive attitude, and explained to him how I get paid for the work I do, and the invoice was the way we keep track of what was done. But he wasn't seeing it that way. His approach was that I was "just" a mechanic, and it wouldn't be any big deal if I would go out to the parking lot and tell him what needed to be done.

You know, the other day I ran into a little problem at the shop. I smashed my pinky finger on a piece of equipment. My wife insisted I have it checked out. Well, I actually chipped a piece of bone along with needing some stitches. I was think-ing..... Why didn't I ask the doctor to just "step outside" and throw in a couple of stitches for me? You know, it's no big deal to the doctor, why he's just a doctor you know.

It's not that I'm comparing myself to a doctor. Oh, by all means I'm not. The comparison is in the respect that is given to the professional in his trade. Not based on what profession it is, the respect that should be given. Needless to say, the fella with the car in the parking lot left, and decided to come back when he had some cash to pay for the work that he needed.

Typical. That's why he wanted to have a tech show him what was wrong with his car in the parking lot.

It's a lot closer to leaving,........ than paying.

HERE, LET ME HELP YOU

Another headlight problem to solve. This time the lady who owned the car insisted on being out in the shop while I worked on it. Normally, with the way the insurance companies are it's not the best thing to be doing. But with my wife in the office and me in the shop, I didn't feel it would be that bad.

It was a late 70's Datsun with no headlights at all. I started under the hood checking the connections and wiring. The owner, who was hovering over my shoulder the whole time, would pick up every tool that was around the shop and would try tightening things on her car, and wiggling things as I was trying make the repair.

Oh she was so helpful. If I was trying get a good ground on my test light, she was right there wiggling the end of the test light connector. If I dropped a tool, she would dash under the car and retrieve it. Now help is great. Overzealous help- now that can be a problem.

I was about at my breaking point when I found the problem with the headlights was not under the hood but under the dash. Not like I wanted to get intimate with some strange lady under the dash, but I could tell if I dove under the dash I was going to have company. Well, I had to go there, you know. If that's where the problem was, I had to get under there and find it regardless.

I made my move. As quickly as I could I crawled under the driver side of the dash. "Click" went the passenger door, and my super helper was right there diving under the dash with me. This was not going to be good. I reached up to the connector for the headlight switch, and I could tell it had been very warm. It was definitely where the problem was. I mentioned to the extreme helper of all times that the headlights might be on now, since I had seen a little spark of electricity jump the connection when I touched it. "I'll go look." She said.

Thanks I needed that. As I was moving the connection around she really seemed intent on watching the headlights blink on and off as I moved it. "They're on..., they're off..., they're on..., they're off." She would tell me.

"Thanks, I've got the problem. All I have to do is make a new splice." I answered.

I guess she didn't hear me, because all I kept hearing for several minutes while I spliced the connections was "They're on..., they're off..., they're on..., they're off." Over and over again.

After awhile I didn't hear my helper anymore. She had walked back into the lobby and told my wife, "I don't think he wants my help out there."

My wife told her, "Well, he can be like that. He gets deep in thought, and doesn't stop until he gets the job done. You're probably better off staying in here until he is done."

I got the job finished up, and the lady paid for the repair. My wife looked at me and said "Why did you leave me with this woman." I was thinking...... why didn't you come out and rescue ME??

I DON'T HAVE
THE MONEY

This is a common occurrence. I probably see this problem more than I care to mention. It happens more likely when you have a vehicle come in with high miles and poor original maintenance. It always comes in with more than one problem under the hood.

I don't know why it always seems to be a referral from a regular customer. I guess the new referral is tired of messing around with other shops, and then finds a friend who keeps their car up. They must figure their friends' mechanic must be better than where they have been taking their car.

That's the first thing this new customer has overlooked. The guy who brings his car in to have it professionally serviced by someone, who spends more time under the hood than themselves, is more likely to have fewer problems. When you let things go, one problem can turn into two, and so on and so on. My old saying is "maintenance is cheap now; not doing maintenance now is going to be expensive later." Where you go can make a difference, but the main thing is ... TAKE CARE OF YOUR CAR! "Maintenance, maintenance, maintenance."

Each time I get into one of these jobs the same thing happens. The final outcome will vary a little, but it still basically the same ending. I'm not going to get paid for the complete job. Only a portion of the repairs get done, based on what the customer thinks is fair. Not the original amount. Oh no, because I must have made a mistake and they know better. (Whatever). I see so many people let their car just fall apart, and then have to replace it. All because it is going to cost too much to repair.

If they would only budget for a continual maintenance or service on a regular basis, a lot of repairs could be avoided. It's the second largest investment in most people's lives. It's necessary to get us from one place to another, and we need them to be reliable. Don't take it for granted just because it's paid for that it still isn't going to cost you more. It will. It is designed to fail. It's not supposed to last forever, but with a little maintenance, it just might.

I'M SELLING THE CAR

I have lost count how many times I have heard this old story. It never fails to end up the same way every time.

In comes a customer with a worn out ride. It's not only in sad shape, but it's on the chopping block. The owner has decided to sell the car, and doesn't want to put a lot of money into it. But, he needs to have it working enough to sell it. So rather than put in good quality parts, he would rather install a cheap, low grade part. I hate doing that, but if that's what they want, well, that's what they get. I had just this type of customer come into the shop the other day.

A rather wore out old jalopy came in with a bad alternator. "I'm selling the car, so can you keep it cheap for me?" he asked.

"I can, but the cheaper part generally doesn't last as long, or perform as well as decent parts do." I told him.

"Well, since I'm selling it, I don't think it matters." He said.

I ordered the part and installed it that day. I have never understood why the cheaper part is so appealing, after you tell them about the risk they are taking. I realize that the almighty dollar is the factor, but what about the professional opinion of the part? Doesn't that have any bearing on the outcome of the repair? I guess not. They decide on what to do, and I do what they want. Hey, I warned them.

About 6 months went by, and I hadn't seen the customer in the shop for any repairs or maintenance on his other cars. I just figured he found another shop to do his work. Just then a tow truck brought the old jalopy back to the shop. It was in even worse shape. The headliner was falling down into the passenger compartment, and it look like somebody was using thumbtacks to hold sections of it back up in place. It had a few more dents, and more oil dripping from the engine. The tires had cord showing through, and the windshield was cracked. This thing is a total "P.O.S" (Piece of S—-). It had even falling part more, since the guy sold it, I figured. I was waiting for the phone call from the new owner of the car, so I could tell him to take it somewhere else. I just couldn't see myself working on this salvage yard attendee.

When the phone did ring it wasn't a new owner. It was the same old customer. He never sold the car, and he was quite upset. "You sold me a defective alternator! It left me stranded at work last night!" he yelled into the phone.

"I sold you what you asked for," I told him. "Do you not remember what I told about the quality of the part? In fact I do recall you telling me you were going to sell this car." After much debate back and forth about part quality, and sell or not sell the car, he understood the dilemma he was in. The cheaper part did have a warranty, but I wasn't going to change it for free. He understood, and paid for the install. I gave him the same old speech on car maintenance that he totally ignored, as he always had in the past. Down the road he went, leaking oil, running on bald tires and holding the headliner up with one hand.

I doubt he has sold the car yet (who would buy it?). I doubt that he has learned his lesson. Every time I hear those words, "I'm selling the car", I tell the customer the same old thing. "Why don't you just leave a blank, signed check on the driver's seat for the new owner to decide what parts they would like to have on their new ride. Putting money into a car you're just going to sell is such a waste of time. Try lowering the price. If you're really going to sell it as a used car, then sell it as a used car. You can always lower the price, and let the new owner decide on what to do. Unless the problem is so drastic that it will hurt the value of the overall car why do it at all.

Cars are sold all over the country with bad motors and faulty parts. I just don't get it. What in the world gets into people's heads to make their used car "perfect" for the next owner? It's like the customer feels they should try to get some value out of all the money they have put into their old ride. It's like they feel it's necessary to drive it around some more, or until the next part falls off. I sometimes think it is the reassuring confidence that a professional mechanic can offer to a customer, who sees his old hunk of junk running like it should, and is just itching to get behind the wheel, and relive all those great moments back when the car was new. But then they forget or ignore the advice of the mechanic, only to confront the problem again when the next failure occurs. Go figure.

YOU CAN KEEP THE CAR

A Honda Passport was the next one on the chopping block. This was another referral from another long time customer. Almost the same thing as the previous story, but like I said, the endings turn out slightly different each time.

This was a dropped off over the weekend, and was sitting there bright and early on Monday morning. A hand written note with the keys was slipped through the first garage door letter slot.

The note had all the needed information on it, but I thought I would wait until I got the call from the owner.

In no time the call came in. A real pleasant type of fella, he was pleased to know his buddy referred him to me, because now he knew his car was going to get fixed. The main thing he was concerned with was the power steering quit while he was driving, and it had over heated at the same time. "Not a problem, I'll get a look at it sometime today, and call you back with what I find."

I DON'T HAVE THE MONEY

When I got out to the car and looked it over, I thought it didn't look like it was in bad shape. Oh, a few little parking lot scratches on it, and a little ding here and there. But with the miles on it, and the shape of the engine compartment you could tell the only thing this owner did to his car was drive. The interior could use cleaning up, but then again, some people just don't worry about those sort of things. Opening the hood was a little bit of a "OH,OH." The serpentine belt was laying on what was left of the tensioner pulley. It was obvious that the bearing had just completely fallen apart, which led to the demise of the serpentine belt. It wasn't long before I got a call back to the owner. "The only thing I haven't done yet is check the water level. I walked out there and saw that the belt was off and the pulley is broken. It's pretty obvious as to what happened to your power steering. Now the overheat situation I can't say what the problem is yet. I'm going to have to get it started to check that out."

"I understand," he said. "Just do what you have to. Call me if it gets into more money."

I got the ok for the work, and went ahead and ordered the parts. While I was waiting for the pulley and belt to be delivered, I decided to check the water level. It was pretty low. Looked to be a gallon or so low. I put some fresh antifreeze into the radiator. Within seconds, the water was running straight down the front of the engine. Crap, the water pump is leaking. Well, I can't go much further now. You have to stop this leak. To make matters worse, the water pump is driven by the timing belt. This isn't a quick fix at all. I called him back, and told him the news. He wasn't too happy, but he understood the dilemma he was in. Again, the dollars were discussed, and an agreed upon amount was set that I wouldn't go over without calling him.

Hey Look! I Found the Loose Nut!

I replaced the timing belt, tensioner, and water pump. I didn't want to take any chances. After all the parts were installed I wanted to see if this thing could start. Cranked the key and it fired right up. Beautiful! Now shut it off, and check the radiator with a pressure gauge. Beautiful! It held pressure. Now it's safe to start it up and let it run. Run it did, for about 10 minutes. Then all hell broke loose. A hose below from under the intake — - shut it down —- now! I called the not so happy customer back. I told him that it was hard to tell, but this might be a sign indicating the headgasket had just let go. Or it could just be an old hose. "Are you sure that when you noticed it over heating you shut it off?" I asked him.

"Yes, I shut it off when power steering stopped, and that was the only time it was hot." He answered.

"Ok, then," I told him. "It's your call, but I think you blew the headgasket. Either way you go with it, it's going to cost more money. Now you can gamble if you like, but I think we should look into replacing the headgasket."

"No, let's just do the hose under the intake. I'm am very sure I didn't hurt the engine any," he answered.

Guess who was right, me or the customer? If you answered customer you lost. After replacing the hose under the intake, the headgasket completely let go. There was no way it "just" over heated. I'm positive there was more to the story. Well, either way it's back to the phones.

One thing to keep in mind, I have never met this man face to face. I know in some parts of the country you have to go in and physically sign a waiver to get any work done. That's actually a good thing. Wish I had that here. When I told him how much the extra work was going to cost, he told me he was out of money. He could pay for the parts but not the labor. I told him that was unacceptable.

He said, "You can just keep the car then."

Sometimes I wish things were more like the medical field. Even with the utmost of care, there is still the risk of the patient dying. When everything all said and done, the hospital still sends you a bill. Terrible comparison, I'll admit. Anybody want to by a car?

4 SALE: Used Honda, slight head gasket problem. Cheap.

YOU'RE JUST ONE OF THOSE SLICK TALKIN' MECHANICS

A referral came in from an old customer. It was an early 90's Ford pickup that could have passed for a clown car. This thing had every color of the rainbow on it. Windshield was cracked, and the driver side window was hanging sideways. Even the bed of the truck was loaded down with all kind of debris from roofing shingles to old busted up lawn furniture. Not to mention the interior could use some house cleaning.

These are the type of vehicles I hate to get stuck behind when I'm riding my motorcycle. You just never know when something is going to fly out of the bed of the truck and smack into you.

The only reason I even took this pile of junk into the shop was because it was a referral from a regular customer. Normally, if you pull up to the shop in this bad of shape you better have one hell of a heart bleeding story, or I'll tell to get it on down the road.

Anyway, this beat up old Ford had so many problems. I had to do my best to sort through what I could. It was hard to start, and when it did start it had a terrible miss. If you tried to drive it even a few feet it would buck and backfire, and eventually start to move, but not without a great effort on the motor's part.

I called our junk collector and told him what I had found right off the bat, and that it needed taken care before we went any further. The old distributor had such a wobble in the shaft that half the time it couldn't find the contact points. I thought this was why it was so hard to start, and for that matter the big backfire. Of course a lot of other things could cause the same problem. But this was so obvious any first year tech could have spotted the problem.

"So that's all there is wrong with it?" he asked.

"I seriously doubt that. I haven't checked it for codes. I haven't looked at the transmission or fuel pressure, but this distributor has got to go," I said.

Now it's a money thing. He told me to go ahead with it, and keep him informed of the results.

After installing the distributor it started right up, even sounded pretty good. Before pulling it out onto road, I thought I better check those codes. There were 2 codes. One for a TPS, and another for the transmission. I called him, and told him what I found.

Now it's back to money thing again. "Ok, go ahead with the TPS. I don't think there is anything wrong with the transmission," he told me. This was like putting the curse of Murphy on the truck. Something has to go wrong now.

I put the TPS in, and cleared the codes. The engine started great, ran terrific, and sounded surprisingly solid. All the codes cleared, and no more really obvious problems (I could have spent days straighten things under the hood, by the way). It was time to hit the road. Oh, oh. The old truck's transmission was trash. Oh, it had all the gears, well, sort of. It would lumber along, drop in and out of gear, and find a new neutral position when it had a chance. For the most part the transmission was in about as good of shape as the rest of the truck. Just plain over worked. You might as well put a fork in this one, because it's done.

Time to make the call. It seems every time you get this far into one of these never ending repairs it will reach a point where you're not solving one problem at a time, but creating an even bigger one, the financial one. Almost every time this type of customer will go along with what needs done until he thinks you don't know what you're doing, and are just out to take their money. Not so! The whole thing comes down to maintenance. It's not like everything broke at once. They let it go, then expect a one-fix repair.

Like I said, the outcome is a little different each time, but the common factor is usually the same. I'm not getting paid for all the work I have completed.....only some sort of agreed upon amount of the repair. This guy took it to the extreme. When I called him and told him about the transmission he didn't have the money. I expected this. Oh, he didn't have the money for the repairs we had already done. What he was going to try to do was talk me into giving the truck back to him, and he would pay so much each week, because he needed that truck to get back and forth to work. If he didn't have a way to work he couldn't pay me. I told him that he should have thought of that before he agreed to the work that was done, because the car doesn't leave until the bill is paid. That's when he started in on me. "You're just one of those slick ass talking mechanics," he shouted through the phone.

"Well that might be the case, and I have been called worse, but we did have an agreed upon bill." I said.

"Oh come on man, I know it didn't need any of that work you did, all it needed was a transmission. So I'm not going to pay for any of it, and I'm picking up my truck today," he screamed into the phone.

Now there are two things to keep in mind on this story. One, he originally agreed to all the repairs as they were getting done. And two, he didn't think there was anything wrong with the transmission. Or did I miss something in this conversation?

The screaming on the phone went on for what seemed like hours. There was no getting through to him about the agreed upon work, or the conversations we had about the additional work to the truck. Or the fact that I had originally told him about the amount of items I found wrong with the truck. I could tell I might as well be talking to the wall.

"Ok fella, I can see were not going to get anywhere. You know me being a slick ass talking mechanic and all. Tell me how much you have, and be honest now. If I agree to accept the amount I'll put your truck out front, and you bring in what cash you have and I'll give you the keys. Here I am trying to help you out, and now all you want to do is change things after the fact. I didn't want to do this job in the first place because of the horrible condition it was in, but another customer said you were an upstanding guy. So I did the work. Take your truck home, and do whatever you want with it, because I don't need to make a living off someone who doesn't trust me. Even if the guy who referred you does.

I DON'T HAVE THE MONEY

He agreed to this strange arrangement, but he was still mouthing off when he got to the shop. He walked out to his truck, and it started right up. He came back in the office still mad as hell, and wanted me to show him which parts I changed, so he wouldn't change the same ones again. I did, and then he wanted a receipt for the parts. Hell, what he gave me didn't even cover the cost of the parts. You can figure out the rest, he left the same way he came in. Unfortunately for him, there was no way to show his manhood with a tire squealing peel out in the parking lot. The transmission doesn't work that well!

Oh by the way, I do feel sorry for the guy, and wish I could have done more for him since he was a referral from a good friend and customer. The money is very important, but I do need to have some assurance that I'm appreciated for what I do. The old customer and I talked about it later. He said he thought the guy was a kind and conscientious guy. He'd never heard a cuss word out him, since he was the janitor at his local church and all. Go figure.

MY REGULAR
"MECHANIC" SAID....

In order to get into this chapter two things have to be present. One, is a regular mechanic who is an idiot. Two, is a customer who believes his regular mechanic really knows what he is talking about.

I guess that makes two idiots per story. Most of the time it becomes an all out shouting match of he said- she said. No matter how you try to explain the problem to the customer, they still insist that their regular mechanic was right and you're wrong.

Even though you have made the repair and the problem is solved, you're still fighting a losing battle with the customer. I usually try to put an end to the confusion by telling them the same story line. "If he really knew what he was doing, then why are you here for me to make the repair?"

The usual response is, "I don't know. You're the mechanic, not me." (It's the first sign of intelligence, and probably the last).

What I found to be true more times than not is the so called regular "mechanic" is a relative or a "Billy-Bob" from next door.

There is the ego issue to tend with. Most people don't want to be shown up, and especially in a trade they feel very well qualified for. The mechanic doesn't want to look bad in front of their customer, and the customer doesn't want to accept that their "regular" mechanic was wrong. Look, everyone makes mistakes, it happens. I get a lot of referral work from other shops because of my background in the electrical side of automotive repair. These guys use me as the "second opinion" and trust my answers; it's the customer who tends to be a little unsure. Sometimes it's a smooth road to be on, other times it's just one pot hole after another. Read on, you be the judge.

"DITTO"

A while back I had the unfortunate luck to run across an old man with two Lincoln town cars. There were several years between the two models. Both cars showed up at the shop on the same day by way of a tow truck. The old fella wanted me to diagnose both vehicles and find out the problems with them.

The first one I went up to wouldn't start. So, now I had to figure out why. Seems it spent some time at his regular "mechanic". The distributor cap was off, ignition module was disconnected as well as a few other important items under the hood. Ok, ok first things first...plug everything back in. (Will someone tell these guys to put the car back the way they found it....please...!) After getting the entire car put back together, I was able to properly diagnose the problem. The compression was very low in the engine. Odds are bad valves, maybe head gasket, rings, etc. etc. etc. Very high miles on the engine; it's probably time for a new one.

Before I called the old timer I thought I better get the other one checked out too. Well now, this one started right up. It actually ran pretty good. I was quite surprised. Next thing to do was to get it in the shop and finish checking it out. Oh oh, no drive. Hell, no reverse. I stuck my head under the car just to make sure there was a transmission still in the car. Yeah, it's there. The fluid was full and looked quite fresh. Something tells me the regular guy has had his hands in this one too. My first guess was the transmission failed, and the mechanical genius decided to change the fluid. Note: fluid color, fluid smell, and fluid viscosity can tell you a lot about a transmissions health. New fluid....well, it's new...can't tell much with that. I would bet to say the front pump went out of the transmission, and that's why it wouldn't pull itself in any gear.

Now it was time to call grandpa, and let him know what I found out so far. Shy of tearing into the one car's engine and the other car's transmission, it would have to be a preliminary guess as to the exact problems, but it's going to be a pretty close diagnosis considering the condition of the cars.

The old timer listened to the diagnosis that I gave him, and he was feeling pretty sure I was right on the button. But that's not what he wanted at all. He already had a pretty good idea it was an engine in the one car, and that it was a transmission in the other one. Now he drops a bomb shell on me. "I want you to take the engine out of the one and put it in the other," he said. "And I want you to take the entire interior out of the one car and put it in the other one. I want the bumpers and grills switched over from one car to the other.

"Well, that's great sir, but that isn't exactly possible. You see there are a few years of technology difference between them, and the parts aren't going to line up. Besides they have two different electronic ignition systems, as well as different transmission control systems," I went on. "I think you would be better off to pick one of the two cars and fix that one, if you can't afford to fix them both."

"Now look sonny!" he shouted. "I'm the customer, and you'll do what I say!"

"Excuse me?" I said.

"That's right sonny boy, you're in business to do what I say. What do think, I'm some sort of idiot!?" He blared out.

"Ahh sir, I don't know where you come from, but seeing how this is my business, I can refuse whatever I don't feel comfortable doing, and this is definitely heading that way", I sarcastically said.

"Oh, you'll do what I tell you too, or I'll see you in court!" the old man belched back.

"Ok fella," I said. "Get out! Your business isn't welcome here!"

"You can't do that!" he said. "I'm a paying customer, and the door is open for business."

"Well, I'll just lock the door and go home then." I yelled back at him.

I think he got the message this time. Out the door he went cussing the whole way. He was already on the phone to his regular "mechanic" yelling all kinds of profanity over the phone by the time he made it to the parking lot. Probably telling his mechanic how we wouldn't do the job the way he wanted it done. By this time my helper was getting the keys for him. The old man stopped him and said, "Your boss is a Horse's Ass. I'll bet he chases work off all the time, doesn't he?"

My helper said to him, "Only those who deserve it, he certainly will."

By this time I was coming out of the shop when my helper yelled back at me, "Hey, this guy says you're a horse's ass!"

I looked straight at the old man, pointing my finger so he would know I was referring to him, and yelled back "DITTO!"

I told this story to a friend of mine who owns an office supply store. A few days later, as a joke to me, he shows up with a pin on button badge with a picture of a horse's ass on it and my name. I guess I deserved that one.

Another "ditto"; another day.

YOU DIDN'T DO A THING

A Chevy pickup with the Anti-Loc brake light stuck on showed up at the shop one day. Not a big problem, but can be an expensive problem to fix. A lot of the replacement parts can run into several hundreds of dollars to well over a thousand for some cars. This customer told me his regular mechanic had already checked it out, and it was going to be so expensive, and take so long to do that he better send it to an electrical expert to have it repaired. (I like this regular mechanic already). After a lengthy conversation with the owner of the vehicle about how long it's been like this,... and how many different parts his regular mechanic had already tried,... and how many times he had checked the fuses,... and that it had to be a huge problem or otherwise his "regular" mechanic would have taken care of it, I put the truck in a bay and put it on the scanner.

Huge or not, I'm the lucky guy who gets to follow up behind his regular mechanic. The previous mechanic had left everything that went to the ABS system unplugged. After getting all kinds of service codes stored in the computer, I had to go back in and reconnect all the different parts. Then I cleared the codes from the computer, and basically started all over again with the scanning and basic testing. (Thank you regular mechanic…you're so helpful). After taking the truck around the block once, the ABS light came back on. Rechecking the codes lead directly to a faulty ABS controller. The controller is basically the brain box that makes the whole thing work. I have changed several of these in the past, and other than the part being extremely ridiculously priced, it's a simple repair. The trick to this one is that the unit is mounted under the car just below the driver's area. If you unbolt the unit and tilt it slightly to the center of the truck, you can get access to the screws that hold the controller to the actual mechanical part of the ABS unit. This way you don't have to undo any brake lines and bleed the brake system. Just install the new one, clear the codes, and do any "re-learn" that needs to be done. Luckily, there wasn't any "re-learn" procedure on this year model.

Okay, job well done, but customer is not happy with the cost. Like I said, it's not the labor that is expensive, it's the part. A few weeks later I get a call from the owner of the truck. This guy was furious. He wasn't holding any words back, and definitely couldn't care less if anybody else was listening. After he was tired of ranting and raving about the repair it was obvious what was wrong. It wasn't the repair, it wasn't the cost….it was his "regular" mechanic. Seems he went over to see his buddy and have some sort of work done. That's when his mechanic told him that it didn't look like we had done a thing, and that he just spent all this money for absolutely nothing.

"Hold on a minute buster!" I said. "Let's start this all over again. First off, is the ABS light off?"

He said, "Well, yeah, it is."

"And is the ABS system working?" I asked.

"It's working like a charm."

"Then what the hell is the problem?" I asked.

"My mechanic looked under there, and said you guys never took the lines off, and didn't replace the controller like you charged me for," was his answer.

I informed him that we most certainly did, because if we didn't your light would still be on and the ABS system would not be working. And further more you don't have to take the lines apart to put on the controller. The controller is the black electrical box above the thing you're calling the lines. As a matter of fact, it's probably the cleanest part under the truck, since it's only been on the car for a couple of weeks.

The customer called back later that day, and was still not buying my story. He did see the new parts, and was aware that everything worked, but... "My mechanic knows you didn't do anything, and you electrical guys know how to jack up the systems to make it look like you did something." He said.

I asked him to let me talk to his mechanic, or bring the truck and his mechanic to my shop, and I'll show them the repairs were made. After the two showed up at the shop I went through the whole procedure in front of them. You could see the light bulb turning on above their heads.

I thought it should have been a neon sign flashing the words. "Dumb Ass", "Dumb Ass" over and over."

I'VE GOT A LIST OF PROBLEMS FOR YOU

A guy brings in this GMC van for repairs one day. He has a huge list of problems that his regular mechanic has written down for him. Of course he has labeled all of them to be one problem and not several small problems. It all started with a so called battery drain. Then there were the wipers that didn't work, and a power window that didn't operate, along with a horn that couldn't make a sound. "He said these were all related, and he knew you are the guy to find out what the problem is", he told me with a smile.

I wasn't so sure they were all related, but I did agree to take on the job and check it out for him. The first thing I ran across was the so called battery drain. It wasn't the van, but an added on power inverter that was draining the battery. The wipers had a faulty ground connection, and the window had a bad switch. The horn on the other hand, was merely a faulty horn.

I called the customer, and told him the results of the tests. The guy was in shock, he just couldn't believe it at all. He was certain I was wrong, and thought it would be better if he talked to his "regular" mechanic, before proceeding with any repairs. So I waited for a return phone call for the "OK" to start on the repairs.

Sometime later the phone rang. It was the "regular" mechanic. A guy I have known for years. I know what kind of work he does. The one thing he doesn't know anything about is electrical systems. His is a brake and engine shop. But it was slow at his shop, and he decided to try his hand at electrical.

I pretty much had to give him a quick lesson on how to do a battery draw test, and how to determine the problem with the wipers. Once he had a better understanding of the procedures, he was even more convinced he shouldn't mess with electrical stuff ,and just send it directly to me. He called his customer, and told him to let me go ahead and make the repairs because it was way out of his league.

I did the repairs, and the customer picked up the car. I do believe I gain a new customer because of it.

Note: If it's not your line of work, don't try learning on a customer's car, or at home in your garage. Cars can be very complicated for something that seems so trivial. Find a book on the subject, or someone who knows how, and see if they'll teach you what needs done to make the proper diagnosis and repairs. As I have always said: "Stupid is free, Smarts will cost you. That's why college isn't free."

SO IF THIS DOESN'T FIX IT

I got a call from one of the many transmission shops that I work with about a Dodge Durango he wanted me to take a look at. He said the customer was probably going to drop it off. They dropped it off early the next day. The problem was that it was in default, or more commonly referred to as "limp home mode," which is exactly the only thing it will do once it is in this mode.

For those who don't know what that is, default is when the electrical system that controls the transmission shifting has shut down, or is turned off. This is due to a failure of either the electrical system or electrical related components that sense the condition of the transmission. In some cases even a "mechanical" break down in the transmission can be detected by the electrical sensors and cause the same "default" to occur.

Once the vehicle is in default it generally will only go into second gear and reverse. The transmission shop said they had checked out the mechanical side, and assured me that it was definitely an electrical problem.

After the Durango limped into the bay, I got it on the scanners and pulled up the wiring schematic on the old Dodge. Between the codes and the wiring schematic, I narrowed down the problem to a lost signal from the computer. After looking up any service bulletins on this problem, I confirmed what I had already figured out. I called the dealer for parts. Got the price....boy howdy! Are they proud of that computer. I know, I know, some of you are saying ... go salvage part....go after market part....check the net. Sorry..... NO! I've been down this road before and found it is a whole lot better with factory parts that have the latest calibrations and updates entered into the computer. There are a lot of good aftermarket parts, but this is one I don't even consider it a good option to try. Sorry after market guys...it's still my shop, and I'm the one who has to deal with the customer if the part fails.

I replaced the computer, got it programmed, and TA DA!! It shifted beautifully. I drove it around in various stop and go's and highway conditions with no signs of any problems, nor any returning codes.

My daughter (who runs the office) called and told the customer it was ready to go. When the owner and her father came to pick it up they had the usual questions like, "how long is the warranty? Where did you get the parts?" Basically your standard — I'm concerned about my daughter driving the car questions. About then I was walking back into the office. All I wanted was a cup of coffee. The dad stops me. His daughter was finishing up with the financial side of the job, and my daughter was just then handing the keys over to the girl.

That's when the dad asks me, "So since this didn't fix it, what are you going to do about it."

"Excuse me?" I asked. "You haven't even left the parking lot, let alone the front office. Have you even driven the car yet? Or, are you saying I didn't fix it?"

"I assume you diagnosed it correctly, and drove it around to make sure it shifted." He replied.

"Yea, that's my job." I answered.

"I've been around long enough to know I should be asking questions." He replied.

"Well, they're good questions, but you sound like you don't trust my diagnosis."

At this point, I realized this guy has gotten to the point of mistrusting everyone who looks at this car. Turns out his regular mechanic couldn't find the problem, and two different transmission shops had referred him to me, so he automatically assumed I didn't have clue what I was doing either.

"Sir," I said, "I assure you that I drove the vehicle, and checked it out thoroughly before calling you and telling you it was finished."

"Well, then I guess I'll have to take your word for it. I'm just asking questions you know." He replied.

"I understand sir, and they are great questions." I said.

I do understand that everyone wants to make sure that the repair was done correctly, and it's the right solution to the problem, but that doesn't mean that everyone is out to "swindle" you. It seems that some people try to make problems where there really isn't one.

We later found out from the transmission shop that the car had a recently rebuilt transmission, and since then the transmission never shifted....until now.

Let's hope the transmission builder did a good job. That's the thing though, even with all the sophistication of the electrical systems, it still relies on good old mechanical parts to make it all work.

I was still a bit miffed by this guy's comments, but the transmission shifted fine. Just because his regular mechanic couldn't do the work, and the transmission shops gave him my name doesn't mean that we are all idiots.

Cars are easier to fix than peoples' perceptions of mechanics.

TAXI ANYONE?

When it comes to businesses like a taxi or delivery company there is usually one common phrase I hear over and over again. "Can you do it cheaper, because I can send you lots of work?"

The truth of the matter, they really don't. Most of these companies (I'm not saying all of them, calm down folks) run every single vehicle as long and as hard as they can. The only way to turn a profit is to keep the vehicles on the road. If they are sitting idle in a repair shop, they're not making money. The last place you'll see them spend a lot of time is in the repair shop. (Keep this in mind next time you get in one). When I do get one of these vehicles in the shop, I do my best to get them done quickly, so they can get back out there and go to work. One other thing common to most of these outfits is the cost. They always want the cheapest deal, no matter what. They always want to bargain, or try to give you some free coupon for some idiotic something or other that you have no need of. But they will try over and over, again and again with the same routine.

I have this one outfit that changes owners faster than a quick lube place can change oil. Since I'm one of the few independent shops who does electrical work, it almost never fails they end up at my door step sooner or later. The latest owner is a real piece of work. He is more arrogant than me, and I thought that was just about impossible. I just don't like this guy. He really gets under my skin, and makes me mad just being in the same room with him.

Well luckily, my daughter was running the front office on this particular day. She took the job in just like any other job. It had a weird problem. The oil warning light would come on any time the brake was applied. Also, on occasions, the engine would just shut off, and when it did the radio would lose all of its prepro-grammed stations. One other thing too, the "key is in the igni-tion" warning buzzer would go off if the drivers' door was opened, whether or not the key was actually in the ignition.

After I pulled the car in the shop I realized I was working on a taxi. The invoice had some sort of cryptic name for the company, which didn't give any clue as to whom or what company I was working with. A lot of the taxi companies come and go, and a lot of times they will use several different names for different vehicles, and not run under the same company name. That's about the time I put 2 and 2 together, and realized it's the same taxi company under a different name. This has got to be about the 5th time I have seen this happen. Oh well, do your job, shut up and go on.

The diagnosis wasn't that difficult. I used a thermal gun to read the temperature of the connections to see if there was anything that might give me a clue. I was thinking right off the bat that it was a loose connection, probably at the battery. Or the chassis ground leads were off. My first guess was right. The negative battery wires were barely connected to the battery post. The thermal reading showed the connector to be extremely hotter than the wires it was attached to. Installing a new clamp and cleaning the area took care of the problem, except for the buzzer issue. That one required removing the key and tumbler and pulling out the broken key buzzer micro-switch.

The whole job was a result of a previous sloppy repair job someone else attempted. The battery clamps were not installed correctly, and the buzzer switch was broken due to the way someone installed the key and tumbler.

I wrote this all down on the customer's invoice. I already knew I was in for a challenge with this arrogant butthead. Sure enough, like he had done in the past, he would be so gracious on the phone, but when it came down to writing that check, he has to make a scene.

When I pulled the car around he was examining the invoice with great care. I handed him the keys, and told him that all of this could have been avoided if the last tech working on the car would have been more careful with his work.

The guy had this strange look on his face. I don't know, I guess I must have shot this guy's dog or something. He started right in on me. "This is costing me too much. Why, my regular mechanic could have fixed this for half this price. I just don't think you want any of my business. Only a complete fool would get his car fixed here."

Man, I couldn't resist, can you blame me? Oh come on.... I had to do it. "Well, I guess you're a complete fool, because I fixed your car." I said. Ok, maybe that was going too far, but it felt so good. I could have sworn I heard a drum and cymbal smash to complete this one liner comedy skit.

It turned out that his regular mechanic was thinking it was something seriously wrong with the electrical system, and didn't want to mess with it. Smart guy. His regular mechanic told him this was the ONLY place to get this kind of work done. (Thanks for the vote of confidence, but I wish you would screen the assholes before you send them over)

Needless to say, I don't do a lot of work for this guy. Not that I'm complaining, I would rather not do any at all. The older I get the more I don't want to deal with people like that. Come on folks, life is too short...lighten up a little. Laugh more, have fun, money isn't everything, enjoy life for what it is. Sure it has its ups and downs. We all have had a bad day once in a while. Just think about this before getting overly angry over something: without a bad day how could you tell the difference from the good ones. Keep that thought in your head while you're taking that next taxi ride. Maybe, just maybe, you'll stop and smile at your ridiculous self. Oh, and don't forget to tip.

INTERMITTENT

What can I say about this subject? It sucks. Never in my life have I seen such antics out of customers than what you will see when it comes to a "sometimes", "once in a while", "I never know when it's going to do it" problem. Nobody, and I mean nobody is going to be happy after these situations.

Typical situation would be the customer calls and tells me that his car died. The tow company drops the car off, and by the time I walk out there and turn the key, it runs like a champ. "It started right off the truck sir. We'll keep it for a while and check it out." An hour goes by, and the customer has already called once or twice. Several more hours go by, and the customer has now memorized the phone number to the shop, and has probably added it to his speed dial. On all his phones. The next morning the phone is ringing as I unlock the shop, and still the car starts. (Do they think I live here? Or do they think I come in several hours before I open the doors and work on their car? Ahhh, that would be a... NO.) The frustration level just keeps building and building. Either the customer is going to get upset to the point of losing control, or I will. Usually me, but I'm not so intermittent.

It never fails to amaze me how pissed off they are when I tell them that it's starting just fine, and there are no signs of any problems. The biggest laugh is when they tell me to drive it home, and feel free to use the car over the weekend if I like, so I can see what it does. Now wait a minute here. When I leave work, I'm leaving the work. Why the hell would I want to take a risk of ruining MY weekend with a car that may have to take a ride on the back of a tow truck Sunday afternoon from the parking lot of the golf course? Hey, I work all week just like you do. Do you like taking your work home with you? It doesn't sound as good now does it? Oh don't worry, when I get back to work, I'll work on the work in the shop. Sorry folks, I don't work at home. I'm like you, when I get home, I would rather do things I want to do. Not work on cars all weekend. Like I said before, I'm not a race nut. I very seldom go to car shows. Don't get me wrong, I like cars, but I'm not a fanatic about them. It's my job, it's my career, and it's a living.

When it comes to these intermittent problems the only person who ever walks away happy in these situations is .... the tow driver.

To explain an intermittent isn't that hard. It just depends on who is telling it. My definition of an intermittent problem is when any circuit or condition does not have a pattern, or logical reoc-currence that can be duplicated, while driving or in the repair shop. Now ask a customer the same thing...... "Well, I don't know when it's going to happen. It did it once yesterday while going to the park, but it hasn't done it today at all." In a customer's response you will almost always have them explain exactly how, when, and where they were when "whatever" happens. But the information that would be important to the final answer isn't forth coming. You have to drag that part out of them.

"Did you drive it far before it happened? How warm or cold was it? Were there any bumps, did you have any accessories on?" The questions and answers can vary from situation to situation, but the main problem is there isn't a problem all the time. That's the problem! How do I fix it if it ain't broke? How do I fix it if you can't tell me what makes it break?

"I don't know, I was hoping you would know," is the usual response.

Before the computer age and the advancements in automotive electronics, the intermittent problem didn't happen that often. Even if they did, each manufacturer had their own little quirks, and it was fairly easy to go through and make repairs. For instance, a Ford with blinking headlights could be a faulty headlight switch. Even though it didn't do it while it was at the shop, it was usually the switch. Take a Chevy for another, blinking headlights on these cars was most likely the dimmer switch. This was a very predictable "intermittent" problem with each manufacturer. Once in awhile, you might get tripped up, but not often.

Now with the multiple circuits and sensor controlled systems, the intermittent problem is an off-the-scale disaster. With electronics heat and vibration are two factors that can determine the outcome of a given failure. And don't forget the oozing mix of chemicals and cold temperatures. Plastics, metals, and fluids can act extremely odd in extreme temperature variations. Ask anyone who has tried to start a car in say, Alaska, or has tried to keep a vehicle in working condition in a high heat, high humidity part of the world. (In certain areas of the world you have to do certain things to a vehicle to maintain it, and keep it ready for the next time you need to use it.)

I guess the point I'm making is how the variety of factors that can affect a given problem in a vehicle is proportional to the weather, vibration, chemicals, and the quality of the manufactured component.

When a failure stops being "intermittent" is when you can actually make a repair. Not before that. Don't let anyone kid you about that. If a mechanic or neighbor says, "Oh that happened to my car. Here's what I did, and it fixed the problem." No matter what they say it's still a guess. Be it a good guess, it's still a guess. Save your money folks, don't start throwing parts at it.

Here's is something you can do to help this situation. Write down when the failure occurs. I generally provide a note pad and pencil to anyone who comes in the shop with an intermittent problem. This way when it does fail they can write down any information that might be useful in making the repair. After several "failures" a pattern will develop, and then a better diagnostics can be made as to what is causing the so called "intermittent" failure.

When you're talking to the technician about an intermittent failure try to avoid using the terms, "Once in awhile, sometimes, now and then, and occasionally does it." What is more helpful would be, how long you had to drive before the failure occurred. What do they gauges read when this happens? Did you make any bumps or turns? Towing a trailer? What were your accessory settings? Avoid the "dog story" it doesn't help, believe me, it doesn't. Stick to what sounds important without getting into your personnel life.

Intermittent failures can be the most impossible to repair. Some will take time to sort out. Other intermittent problems can be solved with the right information. That's where the notepad can help. Take the time, and write it down. You may be surprised how easy it is to solve, once the information is sorted out and a proper diagnostics can be made.

This is an example of the type of questions that can help solve an intermittent problem. Take this note pad to your tech the next time you are experiencing an intermittent type problem.

INTERMITTENT NOTE PAD

Write down anything you think is important for the mechanic at the time of the failure. Here are a few helpful hints for you to follow:

TIME OF DAY

_____

LENGTH OF DRIVE

_____

OUTSIDE TEMP

_____

ENGINE TEMP

_____

ROAD CONDITIONS

_____

ANY PASSENGERS & WHERE SITTING

_____

WHAT ACCESSORIES ARE ON

_____

HOW MANY RESTARTS BETWEEN FAILURE

_____

NOISE OR VIBRATIONS BEFORE FAILURE

_____

GAS GAUGE DILEMMA

A late model Windstar came in with an unusual problem. It had been to several shops and even a dealership. The problem was that at certain times the gas gauge would just start going nuts. One minute it was full, and the next it was empty. Sometimes it would swing back and forth without any reason. Definitely an intermittent problem.

The usual test procedures for the gauge showed everything to be working correctly. That was no surprise, since it's usually working when it's in the shop. I talked with the owner, and gave him the note pad and pencil. He came back in a few days with all kinds of notes scribbled down for me to read.

Sorting through this jumble of information led me to believe that it seemed to have more to do with bumps and cornering. Not every time, but perhaps more often than in any other situation, the gauge would act up. Going through the wiring and data lines on the prints didn't really give any clues. I had to dig further into this one to come up with an answer. By this time I thought I had enough information from the customer to try and duplicate the problem in the shop.

I had a hunch it was the location of the front and rear body control modules. These modules are what interface between the actual gauge on the dash and the sending unit in the tank. I didn't see anything wrong with the front module, so I figured I might as well look at the back one.

The rear module is located directly behind the spare tire mounting brackets on this model year. There was something strange already about this car. My guess is somebody had a flat, and didn't install the jack back into its cradle properly. Well, that's what it looked like anyway. I took the side panels off, and removed the brackets. There was the module, right where it was supposed to be. Nothing looked terribly wrong, except for a very tiny dent in the casing of the module. The dent was in perfect alignment with the large bolt that attaches the jack to the brackets in the car. No way, could this be the cause? I removed the cover to the module, and sure enough the dent was just a fraction of an inch away from the internal circuit boards. I put the cover back on, and plugged the whole thing back in. I then started up the Windstar and left it in park. I went to the back, and ever so slightly pressed on that very spot where the jack bolt had indented the cover. Sure enough, the gas gauge went crazy.

Of all the things it could have been, it was from having a flat and not putting the jack back correctly that caused the whole thing. Once I bent the module's lid back out, the gauge never acted up again.

I told the customer my hunch, and how I proved it. He said the gauge didn't mess up until after they had a flat coming home from vacation. The customer thought it had to do with buying gas in strange places, not the actions of changing a tire.

Note: If the jack doesn't go back in the way it came out, don't force it into place. If the bolt seems to be going in farther than it did before, then don't do that either.

Then again, this repair was simplified by just writing down the sequence of events, and then making the repair. By now there is service bulletin on this very problem. It's no longer an intermittent problem…it's a fact.

COOKIES AND COOKED FUSES

An elderly lady came into the shop one afternoon with a small problem that wouldn't go away. She had a fuse that would blow, and not allow her car to start. The only way it would restart was to replace the fuse and try again. Sometimes it may blow right away,and other times it may go for days and not ever act up again. But, it always seemed to return no matter what was done to the car. She had been to several other shops close to her home, all with the same results. Not one of them could seem to find the problem for her. This poor lady was so confused with all the information she was given from all the other shops. Everything from a strange relay causing the problem to, "Oh I found a shorted wire ma'am, it's fixed now for sure." The last shop simply gave up and handed her a box of fuses with one of my business cards. Now it was my turn to figure it out.

Now there are several "good guess" possible answers that could help in solving this problem. You could take one of those guesses, try it and see if it made any difference, but I prefer (and probably always will) to have the problem right in front of me with some way to repeat the problem....or I would hope to anyway.

The owner was very helpful; she really wanted to get to the bottom of this strange problem. She even offered to go home, and get the blown fuses so I could see them! My concern was not the fuses I needed to see, but what was causing the fuse to blow. The best advice I could give her at the time, considering all that she has been through already, was to take our "intermittent" information page home, and keep track of the failures (a copy is provided in this book). Then I wanted her to bring it back when she thought she had enough information for me.

The following Monday morning she was there bright and early to fill me in on what she had written down. I'll have to admit there wasn't much of a pattern. Not really a whole lot to go on, but there wasn't anything else to do but work with what information she could provide me. Somewhere on that piece of paper was the clue where and how this problem was happening. The problem now was how to be a good enough detective to solve this intermittent mystery. I told her to leave the car, and I would give it a shot and see what I could find.

A day went by and I wasn't getting anywhere. I just couldn't find a connection between how it was happening, and why it would come and go so often. That's when my daughter decided to play the part of a little old lady, and see if she could get the fuse to blow. She walked over to the car and got in it, wiggled around a wee bit, and adjusted the seat, open and closed the glove box, moved the mirrors, anything she could think of that someone would do when they were about to start the car. Each time she would try over and over again. Sure enough the fuse blew. "Ok Mandy, let's go through everything you did, exactly as you did them, while I go over the notes the lady left me," I said.

As Mandy and I went through the scenario, again and again I could see the pattern developing. The problem seemed to be more and more related to when the driver's door was closed. It was the "jiggle" from slamming the door, not the door itself, but something that was moving that was making this fuse to blow. It still took some time to find the actual problem area, but when I did....there was no doubt about it. A year earlier the little old lady had some transmission work done. The transmission was fine, but they didn't put all the harness brackets back in place. One of them was barely up against the exhaust crossover pipe, and ever so lightly touching the hot exhaust. Touching, never the less. The only wire affected was the starter wire that leads to the PCM (Powertrain Control Module, or in other words the computer). This harness of wires is rather large and bulky. I could see how it could, just ever so slightly, swing against the exhaust, and short out the fuse. That's why it didn't do it every time the door was closed, or for that matter every time she hit a bump....just "intermittently". In fact the actual "damaged" area was no bigger than the tip of a ball point pen, but it was enough to cause the whole problem.

The little old lady picked up her car the next day, and was so relieved to have this problem solved. A week or so later she came back into the shop. She didn't need any car repair work done. She had made a batch of cookies, and wanted everybody at the shop to know how much she appreciated the work we had done.

It makes a person feel pretty good inside when you run across a customer who shows how much they really do appreciate what you've done. Ok, maybe it's just because I like cookies. Appreciative customers and great homemade cookies...Ahh, life is good.

THE ONES I REMEMBER THE MOST

These stories are about some of my favorite people in the whole world. Without a doubt, I call these customers my friends. Lifelong friends and definitely the kind of customer I wouldn't mind giving my home number to. Most of them either have their own businesses or work in a retail style business. A few are teachers, principals, golfers, and are just goofy enough to make me laugh out loud. They not only help support my shop with work, but also make my weekends brighter, as well as a beer or two now and then. Some are older, some are younger, but I consider them close friends regardless who they are. If you weren't reading this book, you probably would have never heard about them. I consider their stories just as important as any of the other stories that I have written. Be sure to thank your friends for being your friend when you get a chance. After reading this you might want to do just that.

DAD

Ok my Dad wasn't a customer, but he did work for me for awhile. His story begins on the country farm where he grew up. I know very little about his upbringing. Probably as much as any average kid knows about his own parents' actual childhood. Dad only made it through the 9th grade. Back then in his small community it was more important to get back to the fields than it was getting an education.

He had a brilliant mind, and could figure out most anything. There wasn't a thing he wouldn't try. When I was still in grade school he switched from farming and trucking to steel work. I guess that's how I got started in the steel business. He worked his way from the floor to the foreman's position, and later all the way up to the executive level. Like I said, he was a brilliant man.

The fall out of the steel business in the late 70's early 80's sent a shock wave of layoffs in the small town. The company moved its entire shop to a non-union state, and attempted to keep going. My dad went with them, and as far as I knew things were great. I was already out on my own, and starting my business. With my schedule and his, it was harder and harder to find time together. We phoned each other all the time. It was like we were right next door to each other.

In the late 80's his health was starting to fail, and with that so was his position with the company. Things had to change, so I offered to help him, if he could help me in the shop. He packed everything up and moved out west with Mom and Grandma. It was the best years I ever spent with my dad. Now, I don't advise everyone working with their relatives. It is hard to turn work off at the dinner table, but it's still great to spend time with each other. We played a lot of golf, and did more things together than we ever could when I was younger.

Working with dad was great fun. Watching him walk around the shop wearing his oversize reading glasses was absolutely a riot. He had to use them to see under a dash, but when he would get back up to walk over to a tool box or something, he would forget that he had them on. When his foot was in the air his glasses made them appear closer to him, and the floor looked farther away. Each step was slightly out of sequence with the next one. Then he would stop in his tracks and cuss his glasses, while reaching in his pocket for his regular pair.

One time we had a customer come in needing a driver side window motor replaced. Dad volunteered to do the job. He like these jobs because he could sit down and do them. After he got the job done he would always go in and start up a conversation with the customer. Always the happy guy. My dad and his new found friend finished up the transaction and wished each other well.

About a year later the same old friend showed up for some other work needed. Dad walked up to him with his usual joyous attitude and said, "How the hell are ya fella?" This was my dad's usual "hello" to just about everyone. (Except for the church ladies).

As they were writing up the ticket the customer asked, "If you've got a minute, could you grease all the door hinges too?"

After he was done with the job the customer originally came in for dad decided to do his chummy buddy a big favor and do a super duper job of greasing the hinges. He took each door, applied the grease in all the right places, and then, swing the door back and forth, while standing outside the car to work the grease into the joint.

When he made it to the driver side door and did the same swinging back and forth he heard a loud clunk, clunk, clunk from the interior of the door. Off came the door panel to take a look inside. Why not? He was going to do this super duper grease job, so he thought he might as well take a look at this problem too. To his surprise inside the door was something that belonged to him! Something he had left in there a year ago. His flashlight. Totally embarrassed, but even more glad to get his flashlight back. Dad put everything back together, and went into the lobby to see his buddy. The customer thought the noise in the door was the hinges and that a little grease would have fixed it up. He felt bad that dad had to go into the door panel and retrieve his flashlight. Dad didn't mind at all, he was glad to do it, and insisted on not taking a penny for the entire job.

The customer took me off to the side where dad couldn't see, and slipped me a 50 and said, "Give that to your dad. He's the greatest." I did just that, and I even told dad why. I had to agree ..... he was the greatest.

About a year later an offer back in his home town came in. I was sad to see him pack and move back, but I know he missed his small town life more than anything else.

I had a few chances to see him before he died, but it just wasn't the same as having him to chat with over coffee, before the customers arrived in the mornings. I still remember the phone call one Monday morning. It was dad on the other end of the phone. He told me he was certain he was dying. I thought he was just being crazy dad, you know cutting up and making jokes.

I told him "Right dad, I'll be up next month, and we'll get out and play a little golf." That Wednesday, he passed away.

So you see, he was a very brilliant man all the way to the end. He knew it was his time, he knew he needed to tell me. I'll never be half the man he was, but I keep trying to live up to his level of human understanding. I miss him every day.............I love you dad.....

BILL

Voted best family one year in my home town. This will give you an idea of the quality person he is. He is a highly professional person, and extremely well respected in the community. And what a story teller! You never have a dull moment when he's around. In fact, Bill is the only guy I know who can laugh at his own problems.

Since his college days, he has had this old Camaro in his garage. It's never been restored or updated. It is as it was when he originally bought it. Some time ago he wanted to add a hidden kill switch to it. We both had suggestions as to where to hide the switch. But with his vote counting a little more than mine, he wanted the switch in a position that could easily be reached without moving from a driving position. Bill didn't want anyone to see him lean forward or side to side, just as he was getting out of the car. That way if he took it out somewhere it wouldn't be so likely to be found out, if someone was watching him park the car. Good idea.

THE ONES I REMEMBER THE MOST

Several years later I got a call from Bill. He was broke down at the office with the Camaro, and he was going to have it towed to me. It was one of those busy days when everything had to go correctly to get things done on time. Between appointments and conferences, and several meetings to deal with that day, the last thing he needed was car problems. He wasn't frustrated at all. It just didn't fall into that category of "things that need done today".

Later that afternoon the Camaro made it to the shop. I went through the usual motions of narrowing down the cause of his problem. The very first thing I found was that the starter didn't work. You know, it had been years since I put that kill switch in. I totally forgot about it myself, but it didn't take long before I found out that he had turned the switch to the off position.

Somehow, while getting out of the car he had pulled his umbrella from under the seat, and got it caught on the switch and flipped it off. When he came out for lunch the car was dead. But that wasn't the half of it. A few of his office friends all wanted to take a ride in his classic 69 for a lunch time run. Instead, there are four executives standing in a parking lot with no ride. Well, at least they could get a good look at the car.

I called Bill, and told him what I had found wrong with the car. There was a long pause on the other end of the phone. Then with a burst of laughter he said, "You know, I was telling every-one here that it wouldn't take you long to find out what was wrong, and that it most certainly had something to do with my own stupidity. I'll never live this down at the office."

I can't imagine this happening to a better person than Bill. Bill is a remarkably smart guy, a great father, husband and a friend. To this day he still has to tell everybody who he introduces me to about his kill switch episode. I love a guy who can laugh at himself and takes life in stride.

Bill, buddy, you make me laugh.

DAVE

Dave was actually my next door neighbor. We had lived in the house for some time before we actually met our neighbors. When we met Dave and his family we knew they were special neighbors. I'm not talking about the wave or the occasional "hello". Our families became best friends. Dave and his wife Mary and all their kids consider my family as an extension of their own. Whether it was a Christmas party or 4th of July picnic, you could count on an invite from them. Great people, great friends. Dave and I played golf almost every weekend. The wives would sit around and talk about us (they must have, because I always got that "look" when I came back.)

Once we got moved in and settled, we began to make our house a home. One day I was up in the attic area figuring out how to turn it into a more useable space. Nothing was up there except for a few pieces of wood. I carried them down to the garage and took a better look at them. I wasn't sure what kind of wood it was but I didn't think it was that rare. It was around Thanksgiving time, so I figured it was a good time to make some toys for the kids. I did this for many years for all my kids, Dave's grandkids, and all my employee's kids. I made the girls doll size rocking cradles, and the boys I made little fire engines with little ladders. The wood was just the thing. It saved me a trip to the store, and I was cleaning out the attic at the same time. That's when Dave came over for the weekly golf report. It's important stuff, you know. You have to know which course we are going to play at and who's all going. Dave took a look at my little projects and said in his usual deep voice, "Nice, looks good. I just hope the kids appreciate these little fire engines you made. Why did you make them out of Mahogany?"

I knew it must have been something like that, but not Mahogany! Later that day Dave brought over a notebook with hundreds of veneer sheets in it. He flipped a few pages and came across the type of mahogany. I couldn't believe it, but there it was. So I guess the kids would have mahogany fire trucks for Christmas. My bad. A few weeks later I was working in the garage and I heard Dave dragging something over to me. He had this old piece of Cherry wood for me. "Here, see what kind of kids toys you can make out of this," he said with half a snicker.

We have been friends for a long, long time. We attend each other's birthday parties, and never miss a chance to rib each other about our golf games. Dave says I still owe him a t-shirt. I told him that if he ever beat me at golf I would make him a t-shirt that said "I beat Gonzo" on it. Don't hold your breath there, ol' Dave.

TOM

Tom is probably one of my first customers. The first time I met this poor excuse for a do-it-yourself mechanic he brought in this box of parts. Well, it wasn't the parts that got my attention. It was the amount of Band-Aids he had on his fingers. At the time I just didn't want to ask what the hell all the band-aids were for.

I'd just met the guy. The box contained all the parts to the inside of the driver's door of a late model Cadillac. It turns out that he had tried to repair his own window motor, and he couldn't quite figure out how to put it all back in. I put the door back together for him, and even managed to snug up the loose door panel a bit, so it wouldn't ride on the edge when he closed the door.

Off and on there would be another repair to make on one of his cars. He would eventually get something newer, and retire the old one. One time he came by the shop to get some quick little something done to the car he had dropped off the day before. The one he was driving just quit in my parking lot. I went out front to check it out. It ran fine, it just wouldn't move. "Hey Tom, it looks like this one just lost a transmission," I said. But that was his luck with cars. One thing lead to another, but he always took it in stride.

It wasn't until many years later I found out about the Band-Aids. It was his wife who filled me in on that. Every time he would work on the car or the lawn mower she would be right there with the Band-Aids. One cuss word usually equaled two Band-Aids. It was a running joke with Tom for many years. He's not too proud of it, mind you. But all and all, Tom is a good guy and friend.

I've known Tom now for over 25 years, and I don't think you'll find a better person out there. We have sat around and told war stories over a couple of beers. I think a lot of him. Not only has he helped support my shop, but he has also been there for my family. I know his kids, and he knows mine.

Even though we may not spend every waking hour together, I do think of him as a brother. Besides, who would want to spend that much time with him anyway.....ok, except for his wife. You still might get a "maybe" from her. You're ok Tom, no matter what your wife says about you.

OLD SARGE

I met this great man through his son, who happened to be the driver of that Chevy van from the furniture store that was my very first customer. Sarge isn't his real name, but that's what I called him. He was a retired Marine Corps cook. I met him one day when he came in with a sick Cadillac.

The old Cadillac hardly had any power at all; just as slow and lazy as a snail. I was only in business for a few months, and didn't know anybody. I didn't have any work to speak of, so even though it wasn't an electrical problem (as he originally thought), I jumped right in and found the problem. It was a clogged catalytic converter. Unbelievably, it wasn't even welded in place. I could take off the clamps, and remove it without much hassle. Back then I didn't have a lift to put the car in the air, so I had to do the whole job on the ground. Well, old Sarge just sat there and watched me do the whole thing. I think he was a little suspicious of this skinny little white kid who was hacking away at his car, but he patiently waited, being the good man he was. We got to talking about things, and it wasn't long before he found out that I was also in Marine Corps. Now we had some common ground. We were buds for life, always cutting up with each other.

One hot August afternoon Sarge brought in one of his other cars to get some work done. I had the back door to the shop open, and Sarge steps outside for a little fresh air. I thought I could hear the guy crying or mumbling something, couldn't tell

which it was. I stuck my head around the corner, "Sarge, ah ....
you ok, buddy?" I asked.

He proceeded to tell me how the house he grew up in was
close by, before it became a shopping center. He talked about his
dad and family, and how he hunted rabbits right where we were
standing. It was during the Depression. Hard times, and things
were scarce in those days. How his dad hid a pig in a pit, not too
far from here. Where they kept the corn mash for making moon
shine. I sat and listened to this hardened Marine tell me his life's
story that day, from his first car to how he ended up in the Corps.
I didn't answer the phone, or go up front to see if anyone came
in. I just sat out there in that August heat, drenched in sweat,
listening to this fella tell me his life story.

I'll never forget that afternoon. I'll also never forget how
every time he came to my shop over the next 25 years he would
sneak up on me, and yell in a drill instructor voice, "TEN HUT!" I
would snap to attention just like a good Marine should.
Sometimes, just to get a rise out of Sarge I would purposely hit my
head on the hood of the car I was working on. He got a kick out
of it every time.

Sarge passed away a couple years back. I still think about
him now and then. I hope he's up there hunting rabbits, or something. Maybe he's guarding the gates like every Marine hopes to
be doing when their time comes. Or, he could be just waiting
there to try and surprise me with one more "TEN HUT" when I
show up.

Sarge, I miss having you around the shop.

Murphy's Laws of Auto Repair

1. Never put all your tools away until you have actually started the car, and know everything is in working order.

2. Always take more than one fuse with you, even though you already know one will do the job.

3. If the customer says it will be "an easy fix" plan on packing a lunch, because this is going to take awhile.

4. If the repair is going smoothly, something is wrong. (Drop a tool on the ground, and let it roll under the work bench or something).

5. There ARE such things as a "Monday built car", and a "Friday built car".

6. If the customer is watching, you're probably not.

7. If you have double checked your work and it seems to be right, check it again.

8. There are more phone calls when you take a lunch break.

9. Proper use of a tool only applies when properly using the tool.

10. You're only as good as your last job.

11. Your last job wasn't that good.

12. Mechanics Beer Rule. 9 mechanics and 10 cases of beer = too many mechanics, or not enough beer. Remove 3 mechanics, or add 5 cases (don't worry, it's not a math thing...just keep them happy).

13. The moving parts of an engine are closer than they appear.

14. Don't always trust a hood prop.

15. Things can go wrong, even when you are not doing anything.

16. Things that go wrong, when you are not doing anything, are still your fault.

17. Gravity is your friend, but not the kind that you trust with your brand new Snap-On sockets.

18. Only upset customers call on a Monday morning at exactly opening time.

19. Not answering the phone at opening time makes customers angry.

20. Yes, I live at the shop 24/7. Of course, I'm there at all hours of the day or night.

21. Oil leaks on the shop floor can be traced in 2 different directions.

22. Only the tool you can't find is the one you need right now.

A PERSONAL COMMENT ABOUT THE AUTO REPAIR INDUSTRY

You know, it's kinda funny. When you talk to other profession-als in the auto business, such body shop owners, repair shops, car sales, etc... you get the same head shaking and half hearted smirk that says it all. And that is: people outside of the profession don't have a clue. You think we just walk back there and put fresh paint on your car by way of some sort of magical substance or mechanical apparatus that modern science has provided. Or there is a super, sophisticated scanning device that can detect a future abnormality in your vehicle days, or perhaps months in advance of the demise of said vehicle. All of which is not true. We all know better. The dedication and time spent learning this craft is a measure of years in the trade. It takes a lot of experi-ence to accurately diagnosis, repair, and deal with the always changing environment of the auto industry. Mistakes will

165

happen, and often do, but the major effort of good, honest, and thoughtful service centers is to take care of its customers. Of course, everyone is looking for the best bargain. Even the used car sales lot is going to try to cut corners, or get the cheapest repair possible. Everyone is in this business for one thing.... make money. A lot of shops will use the old ploy, "Oh that last guy you were at is an idiot. We can do the job cheaper and better than he can." Well, just remember.... You get what you pay for, folks. You can't buy used, and expect it to be new. Cheap is not always the best. The expensive shop may have an edge on the competition, or might be more experienced at that certain repair. Cheap parts and cheap mechanics are not a good mix. Customers who feel the best deals are the cheapest deals can likely expect a problem with the repair. The expectations of the customer who wants to use cheap parts usually are much higher than the results of the repair shop's abilities or workmanship. You just can't make cheap parts work like good parts can.

Give us a break people, we can only do so much. Cars are not built to last you a life time. The economy would fall to zilch if we didn't keep the auto industry up and running. Everything we do in this day and age is in some way tied to the motor vehicle. Back and forth to work, going to the store, school, and church. That taxi ride downtown, the school bus to the football game. It's all about cars and trucks. Our country couldn't survive without guys like me and others to make these wonders of technology run down the highways of this land. Every day I study something new on cars and trucks, and every day I keep learning new techniques.

You know, in the medical field the common term that denotes a doctor's business is referred to as a "practice". Somehow I don't think my customers would appreciate my telling them I am just 'practicing". Think about it.

But, the look is entirely different if you are talking to a customer. The intensity and the demeanor say something entirely different. My interpretation of this phenomenon (if I dare call it that) is the "I ain't stupid, but you don't understand." So I'm going to give you this look that says, I understand completely but I haven't a clue if you know for sure what you're talking about. This isn't true all the time, but then again this book isn't about the usual customers this is about the ones who never get the idea they are not thinking clearly. I'm really hoping that after reading this book you will walk away with a different understanding of what it takes to even think about going into private business with the general public as your income. Or for that matter what it takes to stay at your chosen adventure long enough to retire. It would be a miracle if after reading this book a person would change or even try to make a difference when standing in line where he or she sees a person acting stupid or out of control in front of a counterperson, or somewhere that is truly inappropriate ... take a minute... help that person out..... and smack'm upside the head. They probably deserve it.

We are all guilty of this from time to time, and we should be made aware of it. What can make a difference is if we, the people, would step in and tell a person... "Hey, buddy, you're out of line." Less time might be spent with the lawyers and the judicial system if we would just all be more understanding and less judgmental of others before we understand things ourselves.

IS THERE A WAY TO FIX THE RELATIONSHIP BETWEEN THE CUSTOMER AND AUTO REPAIR SHOPS?

The first thing we should talk about is the customer. Customer "BEWARE" should always apply no matter what kind of service is done for them. Whether it's your home or car, or for that matter anything at all. The customer should always be on guard when it comes to their personal property. So how can we improve on that? I truly believe the problem rests with the industry itself. When a consumer needs a service, such as auto repair, they are not concerned so much with the name of the shop that is actually going to be performing the work, but rather one that a friend has referred them too. If they are new to an area they will generally go to either the place near their home, or ask one of the many agencies for their recommendations. After awhile it's not so much the name of the shop that is a concern, but the name of the mechanic and his reputation. Some mechanics stay at one shop for years, some are the owner operator types, and other mechanics will float from shop to shop. It is the mechanic who is the key to the actual repairs, rather than the repair shop. What if there was a way the shop could be rated by way of a monthly, yearly, or occasional spot check with a "bait" vehicle that is purposely setup with a certain failure which then can be evaluated? The entire process from the time the customer enters the repair shop lobby to the time the job is completed could be graded. Something like the health department uses to monitor the condition of a restaurant or food service establishment. A rating could then be obtained to signify the quality of the shop's performance, such as A through D. At that point a posted grading system could be placed at the customer entrance. When a customer arrives at the repair shop they have a better idea of the quality of the work the shop performs. In addition to the ratings a price cap could be put on the maximum labor rate that each level could charge. The parts quality and the quality of the work done at the shop could be monitored at all times. After every re-evaluation the shop could be given a higher or lower rating depending on the outcome. Of course, you would like to hold the highest evaluation you possibly can, and that would depend a lot on the skill of the employees and the quality of the components used in the repair. You could go to any shop and have any work done, but the difference would be the consumer now has the burden on them for their choices. If you go to a D rated shop you would know you are going to get the sub standard parts, and you can just about guess that the guys in the shop may be limited in their knowledge of some repairs. You basically are taking chances no matter where you would go for repairs, but the odds are in the customer's favor to go to the best rated shop they can find. Even with the rating system if something didn't go right with a job an arbitration panel could go between the shop and customer and determine the proper results. It could end up with the shop losing a rating level, or perhaps a complete exoneration from any wrong doing. But at least everything could be on an equal playing field. Mechanics with great reputations for their work would stand out from the rest. Junior mechanics looking to apprentice in the business could easily seek out the best in the business.

I feel the independent repair shops will always be around regardless of how sophisticated the automobile becomes. Shaping up the independent shops so there are fewer "fly by night" shops and shady business practices that give the entire industry a bad name, could be somewhat controlled, and/or completely eliminated. I'm not for "big brother" watching over my work or work area, but something should be done in order to keep the honest shops and techs in business, and making the consumers aware of who is doing the right stuff. You don't have to agree with me on which way is better to solve this problem, but if it at least makes you think of alternatives .... Well, then I've done my job.

MY CLOSING THOUGHTS

What have I learned from my nearly three decades in the automotive repair business? What will I take away from all this? Plenty, and proud of it. As my business has grown from its meager beginnings, so has my awareness of the nature of people and their frailties. The challenge of the ever changing automotive field has been an uphill climb to stay in business to say the least, but I'm very proud of what I have accomplished. Over the years I began to feel like I have become a bitter, uncaring individual, but I know now, that's not entirely true. When you deal with people and their cars all day long it's hard not to become irritable or uncaring. I struggle daily with this. The real nature to the human being I call myself is being self aware of who I am, and what I do. Being proud of what I do, and not be so judgmental of others is what I have learned the most. I can sit back and laugh now at how I would have handled some situations in the past, if I only had this book to enlighten me on what to expect. I probably would have done things differently. I just hope that after reading this you too can see the humor in the situations you have or will come across.

I have met so many wonderful people in my daily adventures. I feel I am truly blessed. Each day when I meet someone new I feel like I have just found a new friend, and they have stories to tell just like I do. I feel very fortunate to listen to them. There are so many other stories I could tell you, and maybe someday I might just do that. You see, every day is another story to be written down, and another day to reflect on human nature. I enjoy reading about people and their adventures. I find it quite compelling to hear about the daily struggles of society, and how we as human beings cope with those situations.

Not everything is easy, and not everything has a clear answer. Sometimes we have to search for the correct answer. Many times it just isn't that clear, and when it isn't that clear, don't get upset, don't get all riled up and want to take it out on somebody else. Learn to except the challenges, deal with them as they come. Show some respect to your fellow man, and try to be honest with yourself and others. Life is what you make of it.

BIOGRAPHY

I wouldn't come close to calling my life a rags to riches story in the least, but it has its moments. I still have a hard time believing how I got to where I am. I was born and raised in very rural Pennsylvania. I lived on a farm, raised animals, and sometimes tinkered around on old cars in my grandpa's shed. I also walked barefoot for miles in the freezing cold through the snow on my way to school, once having to fight off a bear that tracked me down for my lunch bag full of peanut butter and jelly sandwiches. Well maybe that last one was a little exaggerated, but I've told my kids that for so long I just had to put it in.

Growing up in the country had its advantages. There is what you would call street smart, and there is school smart, but living in the country you tend to be more common sense smart. On the farm or out in a field you had to be able to keep the machinery moving and productive, and that's where a lot of my early skills were developed.

Hey Look! I Found the Loose Nut!

After an honorable discharge from the United States Marine Corps I eventually ended up in Oklahoma. I worked in the Tulsa steel industry on and off for a few years, but between each layoff I would put my background skills in automotive electronics to work. As the layoffs became larger and longer than the last, I had the crazy idea to open my own repair shop.

I saw a need for my skills in automotive electronic repair. I knew that I was good at it, and understood the basic mechanics of the systems. I also knew I could learn more as I went along. What I didn't know, was how to run a business. I found a space to rent that had a decent sized shop, big enough for two cars, three if I tried hard, and a small, but efficient office/waiting area. I had a handful of tools and what some might call enough stupidity to make this whole thing work.

What may have been through divine means, or probably more an ironic coincidence I opened my doors to the public April 1st. It's as if my life's direction with my shop was destined to be one big April's Fools day, one Murphy's Law away from a self-committed trip to the looney bin. In reality, it's just one big adventure. Customers and their cars came and went. Starting out I never imagined what kind of effort and time it took to make a successful business thrive, but here I am nearly 30 years later, with a whole lot of stories to go along with it.